In memory of the sweetest perfume, my father,
Ilhan Mehmed Lautliev (1925–2007).

Purple Citrus
& Sweet Perfume

Cuisine of the Eastern Mediterranean

Silvena Rowe

With a foreword by Heston Blumenthal

Photographs by Jonathan Lovekin

An Imprint of HarperCollinsPublishers

FIRST PUBLISHED IN GREAT BRITAIN IN 2010 BY HUTCHISON, RANDOM HOUSE,
20 VAUXHALL BRIDGE ROAD, LONDON SW1V2SA.

HarperCollins books may be purchased for educational, business,
or sales promotional use. For information please write:
Special Markets Department, HarperCollins Publishers,
10 East 53rd Street, New York, NY 10022.

FIRST U.S. EDITION

Designed by Richard Marston

Library of Congress Cataloging-in-Publication Data has been applied for.

ISBN 978-0-06-207159-0

11   12   13   14   15   DIX/C&CO   10   9   8   7   6   5   4   3   2   1

Contents

Foreword by Heston Blumenthal

When Silvena asked me to write a foreword to her book, I couldn't help but say yes. Everything she does, be it writing, broadcasting or cooking, she approaches with the same boundless energy and enthusiasm, and her infectious passion is impossible to resist. She has written books and columns, presented television shows, been a consultant to top restaurants and cooked for an impressive lineup of celebrities, and each project is connected by her individual brand of dedication and her original take on food.

As a chef, I find other people's food memories fascinating, and *Purple Citrus & Sweet Perfume* is full of stories and reminiscences that set it apart from most cookbooks. Silvena's nostalgia for the aromas and flavors of her childhood really brings the recipes alive, and the book gives us a very personal glimpse at the relatively unexplored food cultures of these Eastern Mediterranean countries.

Her Eastern European heritage gives Silvena a unique perspective on this part of the world, particularly through her father and paternal grandmother, who were of Turkish descent, and it is fitting that she is our guide to the unfamiliar dishes, exotic spices and new ingredients of these cuisines.

As well as the food of her childhood, there are more recent discoveries from the restaurants of Damascus and the cafés of Istanbul, and more traditional dishes from the kitchens of the Ottoman Empire. In fact, this stunning book is part travelogue, part memoir, part history lesson and part cookbook. It is beautifully written with a rich mix of evocative stories, poetry, fairy tales and history, woven into the carefully crafted recipes, and the fantastic photographs add to the seductive atmosphere captured by the words. Furthermore, the pages are so packed with Silvena's characteristic enthusiasm and irresistible passion, I defy anyone to resist.

Introduction

In the early part of the twentieth century, when the latest medical breakthroughs were finding their way into the back streets of old Damascus, an elderly blind woman underwent a cataract operation, and afterwards, when she was recovering and the bandages were removed from her eyes, she was asked by the doctor what it was that she could see. "I can see your face," she replied.

These plain and simple words serve to underline what I hope to achieve with this book. To open your eyes to the cuisines of the Eastern Mediterranean, to allow you to see and taste for yourself the wonderful panorama of fruits, vegetables, meat and rice dishes that this region has to offer; to wander through the kitchens of Turkey, Syria, Jordan and Lebanon, the cuisines of Europeans and Arabs, of Muslims, Christians and Jews, discovering as we go the old world of the Ottoman Empire.

For 500 years the Ottomans ruled what is modern-day Bulgaria – where I grew up – leaving only in the latter part of the nineteenth century. What followed was, in culinary terms, a black hole.

At the very zenith of their power the Ottomans controlled not just the Eastern Mediterranean, but most of the Balkans, much of the Caucasus, the Crimea and the Middle East. The cities of Athens, Budapest, Belgrade, Sarajevo, Bucharest, Sofia, Beirut, Damascus, Baghdad, Jerusalem, Mecca, Cairo, Alexandria, Tunis, everything to the very gates of Vienna, fell under the Sultan's power.

The Ottomans were no stick-in-the-muds – as their armies rolled through the neighboring countries they embraced the local cultures and, more important for this book, the local cuisines. The vast tracts of land over which they held sway offered unmatched fertility, and, just as the sun never set on the British Empire, so it is said that the fruits and vegetables of all seasons could be found in the markets of Constantinople (the Ottoman capital and now modern-day Istanbul), such was their all-encompassing power.

The entire region became a melting pot of cuisines, bringing a mélange of tastes, colors and smells. Chefs were invited (or enslaved) from across the Empire and beyond, and Armenian, Greek, Persian, Egyptian, Serbian, Hungarian and even French chefs came to Constantinople, first to the Sultan's Topkapi Palace, then to the homes of the fabulously wealthy. Even the Spice Road, the most important factor in culinary history, was under the Sultan's control. So only the best ingredients were allowed to be traded under the strict standards established by the courts, which meant recipes of unparalleled flavor could be produced. Consequently, a grand gastronomic tradition was

developed by the aristocratic elite of the city, a culture that covered everything – the ingredients, the methods of cooking, the kinds of food, the kitchens and even the table manners – and spread to the farthest regions of the Empire.

In its heyday the wealth and splendor of the Topkapi Palace were renowned across the world. The gardens, courtyards and vistas, the glittering domes and minarets, the baths and marble fountains, the carpets, textiles and ceramics, the paintings, the jewels, the objets d'art. The swords, the hair plucked from the beard of the Prophet, the Holy Mantle and other relics of Muhammad brought from Mecca, the Meissen and Limoges porcelain presented by European royalty, the great fireplaces, the thrones, the Iznik tiles in all their brilliant colors. The sea-view windows encased with mother-of-pearl shutters.

The Ottomans, open to all the sensory delights, were absolutely crazy about haute cuisine, and the vastness of their kitchens almost defies comprehension. Housed under ten domes, at their height the Topkapi kitchens employed 1,300 staff. Hundreds of cooks, specializing in different categories of dishes – soups, pilafs, kebabs, vegetables, fish, breads, pastries, sweets, helva, syrups, jams and beverages – fed, on feast days and special celebrations, as many as 10,000 people a day. The Sultan had his own personal staff of seventeen specialty chefs and still more for his family. His food was prepared with great ceremony, and never consisted of fewer than twenty separate dishes. Each dish was brought in one at a time, covered and sealed with a ribbon to prevent it from being poisoned.

Following the example of the Palace, all the grand Ottoman houses boasted elaborate kitchens and competed in preparing feasts for each other as well as for the general public. In fact, in each neighborhood at least one household would open its doors to anyone who happened to stop by for dinner during the holy month of Ramadan, or during other festive occasions. So it was that the cuisine evolved and spread, even to the most modest corners of the Eastern Mediterranean.

It would be impossible to cover every cuisine deriving from the Ottoman Empire, so I have stuck, with the odd sidetrack, to the eastern end of the Mediterranean. Here you will find a modern twist on the classic recipes of this rich culinary tradition, following in the footsteps of the great Ottoman chefs who combined the sweet and the sour, the fresh and the dried, honey and cinnamon, saffron and sumac, scented rose and orange flower waters with the most magical of spices. This book is proof, if proof were needed, that there is a lot more to the Mediterranean than just Italy and France.

Chef's Note

All **herbs** listed in the ingredients are dried, unless otherwise stated. When using fresh herbs, most of the time you can use as much as you wish to bring the flavor out.

When it comes to **olive oil**, I always use the best-quality extra virgin oil I can find, as this will always have the most satisfying flavor. But it's fine to use whatever olive oil you have on hand. I also often recommend cooking with clarified butter, also known as **ghee**, which you can make at home or buy in jars at Indian grocers, as it doesn't burn as easily or turn brown.

I **season** a lot of my dishes with freshly ground sea salt and black pepper. Always use as little or as much as suits your tastes.

At the end of the book you'll find a useful list of **pantry essentials** appropriate to the recipes in this book. It includes the simple recipes for two classic Eastern Mediterranean spice mixes that I often use – za'atar and baharat – which are both also available to buy prepared. It also features easy instructions for making pomegranate molasses, another Eastern Mediterranean staple. Za'atar, baharat, pomegranate molasses and other Eastern Mediterranean ingredients are readily available at Middle Eastern grocers and online at www.akmarket.com and www.kalustyans.com.

Hakawati Abu Shadi: The Last Storyteller

Early one morning I left the center of Damascus and traveled east, thirty kilometers out through the suburbs, where the remnants of olive, lemon, pomegranate and orange groves and ancient farmhouses can still be glimpsed. As we neared our goal, the home of Abu Shadi, the apricot, cherry and apple orchards asserted themselves. Even for my driver, a resident of the old city, this was an adventure, and I asked him if he knew of the Hakawati.

"Where I live," the driver replied, "everyone is a Hakawati, everyone tells stories, and we do not need books." A Hakawati is a storyteller, and Abu Shadi is the last Hakawati in Damascus – some believe that he is the last Hakawati in the whole of Syria. There is no greater tradition in Syria than that of storytelling.

Abu Shadi was born and raised in the center of the old town. From eight years old, he would go with his father to the Al-Nafurah Café, next to the grand mosque, and listen, fascinated, as the Hakawati of the time told his tales. Every day he would go, and when the Hakawati finished, Abu would beg to be given the Hakawati's book to look at. When Abu was twelve years old, his father died, but as the café owner was a close family friend, he was still welcomed and became like a son to the café owner.

The last of the old Hakawatis passed away in the seventies and Abu Shadi was asked if he would take on the mantle at the Al-Nafurah. He was unsure—times had changed, there was a television in every home, competition to the old ways. But the café owner was persistent, insisting the people still wanted a Hakawati, and in particular they wanted Abu Shadi. Only he knew the language in which the stories must be told, the style, the content. Finally he agreed.

"As I sat on the Hakawati chair the café was full, the sweet smell of apple-flavored hookah tobacco in the air, the expectant faces of the patrons," Abu recalled. "I was trembling, my heart beating fast. I wanted to run, but all were looking at me, strong eyes that encouraged me to begin the tales."

At first Abu believed that his style was too wooden, his narrating skills but a poor imitation of those Hakawatis that had gone before. Not long after he began, a famous Lebanese actress came to the café to listen to him. Afterward they were introduced and Abu decided to ask her advice. She told him that if she had a stick, she would beat him with it. He was astonished and asked her why. She told him that he was merely repeating the words, he did not look the people in the eye, did not convey the passion of the story. So she took the book and she showed him how to act and use his body language. Abu told me he would have been nothing without her help. She invited him to Beirut and showed him how to use the tone of his voice, to move his body, his hands, his arms, his legs, each movement to convey meaning and emotion. These were the most important lessons he ever learned.

As we sat in the garden of Abu Shadi's home, he told me the beginning of a tale, that of Prince Antar and the beautiful Abla, her "face like the moon, lips like peanuts, nose like a noodle, cheeks like Syrian apples, eyes like a gazelle, hair like a long strand of silk." This was Abu's first story as a Hakawati, and he returned night after night to tell it at the Al-Nafurah. For the hour between prayers, he would enthusiastically embellish, bang his flat sword in his hand, switch from voice to voice, and repeat key phrases in several languages so that all his audience would understand.

Much as I would like to include the tales that Abu Shadi tells, they would be far too long, for they are tales of truly epic proportion, stories of a great people renowned for their chivalry, truthfulness and generosity. Tales that can quite literally take a year in the telling, as they're entwined with anecdotes, comments and adaptation for modern times. But they never lose sight of whence they came. Likewise I have done just so with these recipes, adapting and changing a classic cuisine for modern times and modern ingredients, just as the Ottomans themselves moved with the ever-changing tides.

MEZZE

In the time of Sultan Selim, there lived in Constantinople a drunkard, perhaps the only one in the whole of Turkey, and as a consequence his behavior was discussed in both high and low society.

The Sultan, hearing of this man, called him to the palace and demanded to know why he disobeyed the Prophet.

The drunkard replied that alcohol was a benefit to man, that it made the deaf hear, the blind see, the lame walk and the poor rich.

The Sultan, wishing to find the truth of the matter, sent his servants to find four men so afflicted; thus found, they were brought to the palace and each was served raki. Before long, the deaf man announced, "I can hear the sound of great rumbling!" The blind man replied, "I can see him; it is an enemy that seeks our destruction!" The lame man said, "Show him to me and I will dispatch him!" and the poor man said, "Do not be afraid to kill him, for I have his blood money in my pocket."

As these things were being said, a funeral happened to pass the palace. The drunkard called from the window for it to be halted, rushed outside and opened the lid of the coffin. He spoke to the dead man and leaned down to hear his reply. Then the funeral went on its way.

"What did you ask the dead man?" asked the Sultan. "And what did he say?"

"I asked him where he was going, and of what did he die. He told me that he was going to paradise and that he had died of drinking raki without a mezze."

Adapted from *Told in the Coffee House*, stories collected in Istanbul by Cyrus Adler and Allan Ramsay (1898)

Mezze

Mezze is about spending time together, enjoying long warm evenings with family and friends, sharing anecdotes and stories of life over a leisurely meal. The Eastern Mediterranean mezze brings together a glittering array of dishes: rustic bean and mustard green salads, velvety tahini-based hummus and smooth vegetable purees, crunchy falafels and the wonderful flavors of crimson beet and emerald-green spinach. Not to mention the sophisticated sumac- and za'atar-flavored seafood and delicately baked pastries accompanying pomegranate and walnut salads enriched with nigella and sesame seeds, all topped off with the cooling texture of natural yogurt. The list is endless, but it is not just about the food as nourishment and satisfying your belly; it is about the colors, the textures, the combinations – a true feast for the eyes.

Mezze is in general an extremely healthy way of eating, combining as it does the most simple and basic of fresh ingredients, making it perfect for the twenty-first-century stomach. So enjoy it for breakfast, as a snack, for lunch or for dinner. To my mind there can be no particular order to a mezze – hot can be eaten with warm, vegetable with meat dishes, it is whatever you want it to be. My personal preference would be something like this: a combination of veggie-based tzatzikis, veggie-based hummus, then falafels, seasonal herb salads topped with white cheeses, followed by stuffed vine leaves, kofte, and finally okra cooked with fresh tomatoes, and a crispy börek.

Suzme Rolled in Za'atar, Sumac and Pistachios

Suzme is drained yogurt, known in the Middle East as labne. When yogurt is drained, and the whey drains away, it becomes very thick. Left for twenty-four hours, it takes on the texture of cream cheese, thereby allowing it to be rolled in a variety of coatings, such as herbs, nuts and seeds. For this recipe you will need to use a good-quality, whole milk, plain yogurt without additives.

Za'atar is a typical Middle Eastern blend of herbs and spices. It is available ready-mixed at Middle Eastern grocers, but it is also very easy to make at home (page 249).

FOR THE SUZME

- 1 quart whole milk plain yogurt, not Greek-style
- 7 ounces goat cheese
- ⅓ cup finely chopped pistachios
- ⅓ cup finely ground pistachios
- 2 tablespoons Za'atar (page 249)
- 2 tablespoons crushed sumac
  sea salt and freshly ground pepper

- 2 pieces of cheesecloth approximately 12 × 12 inches
  wild greens, for serving
  warm crusty bread, for serving

1 or 2 days in advance

To make suzme, place the yogurt in the center of the double-layered cheesecloth. Standing over a sink, twist the muslin around the yogurt until you have a tight ball. Tie the top with some string and suspend the ball (I tie it to the tap) overnight. You will end up with yogurt of a very thick consistency, which is known in the Eastern Mediterranean as suzme. You will have about 1½ cups (11 ounces). Cover and refrigerate for 2 hours or overnight.

On the day

Place the suzme in a bowl with the goat cheese and combine until smooth. Put aside about 2 tablespoons each of the chopped and ground pistachios.

Shape the mixture into thick ovals, using a generous teaspoonful at a time. Roll a third of the ovals in the za'atar, coating each one generously, and put to one side. Repeat this with the remaining ovals, rolling half in the sumac and the other half in the pistachios. When making the pistachio ovals, for variety of texture, you can do some with just the ground pistachios, some with just the chopped pistachios and some with both.

Arrange all the ovals on a platter, sprinkle with the remaining pistachios, season and serve with wild greens and warm bread.

SERVES 8

Crispy Spiced Shrimp
with Avocado and Tahini Sauce

1 large ripe avocado, peeled and
   pitted

grated zest
   of 1 lemon

3 tablespoons lemon juice

2 tablespoons olive oil

1 tablespoon tahini

1 garlic clove, minced

   sea salt and freshly ground
   pepper

FOR THE SHRIMP

2 tablespoons all-purpose flour

2 tablespoons semolina

2 tablespoons black sesame seeds

1 teaspoon ground cumin

1 teaspoon crushed sumac

1 teaspoon ground ginger

1 teaspoon ground coriander

12 jumbo shrimp, shelled and
   deveined

4 tablespoons olive oil

To make the sauce

Combine all the ingredients in a food processor and pulse to
puree.

To cook the shrimp

Preheat the oven to 200°F. Combine the flour, semolina, black
sesame seeds, cumin, sumac, ginger and coriander in a bowl, then
season with salt and pepper. In a separate bowl, cover the shrimp
with 2 tablespoons of the olive oil.

Heat the remaining olive oil in a nonstick pan. Dip each shrimp in
the flour and spice mixture, coating them well. Sauté the shrimp
for 2–4 minutes in the pan, a few at a time, until golden brown.
Keep each batch warm on a baking sheet in the oven.

Season the sauce and serve with the crispy shrimp.

SERVES 4

Haydari – Yogurt and Feta Dip

Haydari is a thick and voluptuously creamy dip made with drained yogurt (suzme). This is something that I vividly remember from my childhood, forming part of a wonderful breakfast served with freshly baked bread. My mother made her haydari with homemade yogurt, adding chopped olives and a hint of olive oil, but my favorite version is this one, using feta cheese and sweet paprika. Make your own yogurt if you've got the time, but otherwise store-bought Greek yogurt works almost as well.

4	**ounces feta, crumbled**
1	**cup Suzme (page 22)**
2	**garlic cloves, minced**
leaves of 6	**fresh mint sprigs, finely chopped**
	freshly ground pepper
2	**tablespoons finely chopped walnuts**
½	**teaspoon sweet paprika**
1	**tablespoon olive oil**

Place the feta in a bowl and mash with a fork. Add the suzme, garlic and mint, and combine well. Season with black pepper.

Serve sprinkled with the walnuts and sweet paprika, and drizzled with olive oil.

SERVES 6

Tahini, Lemon and Sumac Sauce

3	**tablespoons tahini paste**
1	**teaspoon ground cumin**
juice of 2	**small lemons**
2	**garlic cloves, chopped**
	sea salt and freshly ground pepper
½	**teaspoon crushed sumac**
2	**tablespoons olive oil**
1	**teaspoon black sesame seeds**

Mix the tahini, cumin and the lemon juice in a bowl. Slowly stir in 1–2 tablespoons of water, a little at a time, until you have a consistency that resembles thick cream. Then add the garlic, and season.

Combine the sumac with the olive oil and drizzle over the sauce. Sprinkle with sesame seeds and serve, with meat, poultry, vegetables or falafel.

SERVES 6–8

Stuffed Vine Leaves with Winter Squash, Rice and Pine Nuts

FOR THE VINE LEAVES

50 fresh or preserved vine leaves

FOR THE STUFFING

¼ cup olive oil

1 large onion, finely chopped

1 pound butternut squash, peeled, seeds removed, finely cubed

⅓ cup Arborio rice

½ cup pine nuts, toasted and roughly chopped

8 sprigs fresh oregano, leaves finely chopped

8 sprigs fresh tarragon, leaves finely chopped

sea salt and freshly ground pepper

TO SERVE

1 cup yogurt

grated zest and juice of ½ lemon

1 tablespoon olive oil

sea salt and freshly ground pepper

To prepare the fresh vine leaves

Select the 40 best leaves and set the remaining 10 leaves aside. Bring a saucepan of water to a boil. Add the leaves and cook 30 seconds for preserved leaves and 5 minutes for fresh. Drain and pat dry with paper towels.

To make the stuffing

Heat the olive oil in a deep pan over a medium heat and sauté the onion for 3 minutes until just translucent. Add the squash and cook for 5 minutes. Add the rice, combining it well with the other ingredients, then stir in the pine nuts, oregano and tarragon, and season. Cook for 10 minutes to parcook the rice.

To make the parcels

Lay out a cooled, blanched leaf, shiny side down, and place a small amount of the squash mixture in the center – just enough to comfortably wrap the leaf around the mixture. Fold the bottom edge nearest you over the filling, then fold in the two sides and tightly roll away from you into a neat parcel.

To cook the vine leaves

Line the bottom of a medium-sized saucepan with 4 or 5 of the reserved unblanched leaves. Arrange the stuffed vine leaves, seam side down, in the prepared saucepan, keeping them nice and tight in layers. Arrange the remaining unblanched leaves on top of the stuffed parcels. Add just enough water to cover. Weigh the parcels down with a plate to keep them in place. Simmer over gentle heat for 45–50 minutes.

To serve

Combine the yogurt, lemon and olive oil, and season. Serve the stuffed vine leaves warm or cold, accompanied by the lemon and yogurt sauce.

MAKES 40

Eggplant, Aleppo Pepper and Pomegranate Spread

This peppery spread is wonderful as an accompaniment to any meat dish, or just slathered on bread and eaten on its own. Aleppo pepper is mild, sweet, fruity and slightly smoky. You might have to look around for it, but it is available dried in many Turkish and Middle Eastern food stores. If you have trouble finding it, substitute a large pinch of mild red chili flakes and a teaspoon of smoked paprika.

The city of Aleppo is in northern Syria, and is claimed to be one of the oldest inhabited cities in the world, having been founded more than 3,000 years ago.

1 **large eggplant**

3 **tablespoons olive oil**

1 **teaspoon crushed Aleppo pepper**

1 **garlic clove, minced**

½ **teaspoon ground coriander**

½ **teaspoon ground allspice**

2 **ripe tomatoes, finely chopped**

2 **teaspoons Pomegranate Molasses (page 249)**

seeds from 1 **small pomegranate**

3 **tablespoons finely chopped fresh cilantro**

sea salt and freshly ground pepper

grated zest of ½ **lemon**

Wash and trim the eggplant, then slice thinly.

Heat the olive oil in a heavy nonstick saucepan and add the eggplant slices a few at a time, cooking them until golden brown. Stir in the Aleppo pepper, garlic, coriander and allspice. Don't worry if the eggplant breaks up. Add the chopped tomatoes and pomegranate molasses and simmer on low heat until the liquid is almost gone and the eggplant is soft and mushy, about 20 minutes. Transfer to a bowl and allow to cool.

Add the pomegranate seeds and cilantro to the cooled mixture, combine and season to taste. Sprinkle with the lemon zest before serving.

SERVES 6

Syrian Za'atar Bread with Thyme Flowers

Breads are an essential part of the mezze table. Traditional breads, especially flat breads, were baked in a clay oven known as a taboon, *where a disk of dough would be stuck against the oven wall and within 1–2 minutes it would become deliciously crisp on the outside and velvety and soft on the inside. This bread is exactly that, a flat bread, not that dissimilar to pita, but flavored with za'atar and baked indoors.*

FOR THE DOUGH

- ¾ cup warm (105° to 115°F) water
- 1 tablespoon active dry yeast
- 1 cup plus 2 tablespoons warm (105°F to 115°F) milk
- 4⅔ cups all-purpose flour
- 2½ cups whole wheat flour
- 2 tablespoons Za'atar (page 249)
- scant ½ cup olive oil
- 1 teaspoon sea salt

TO SERVE

- 2 tablespoons fresh thyme flowers

To make the dough

In a bowl, combine the warm water and yeast and allow to stand for 10 minutes, by which time it will be foaming.

Add the warm milk to the yeast mixture. Sift the all-purpose and whole wheat flours into a separate large mixing bowl and make a well in the center of the flour. Add the yeast mixture to the well and stir to combine. Then knead the mixture into a soft, sticky dough. Shape the dough into a ball, place in a flour-dusted bowl, cover with plastic wrap, and allow to rise for an hour.

Preheat the oven to 475°F.

When the dough has risen, punch it down once with your fist to knock the air out of it. Cut the dough into 16 pieces, rolling each piece into a ball. Using a rolling pin, flatten them into disks, 5 inches in diameter. Arrange the disks on baking sheets, cover with plastic wrap and allow to rise for 20–30 minutes.

Mix the za'atar with the olive oil and drizzle over the risen dough disks. Press the disks down with your thumb and season generously with the sea salt. Bake on the baking sheets for 4–5 minutes, until they puff up, keeping a close eye on their progress, as the bread can burn very easily.

To serve

Sprinkle with the fresh thyme flowers and serve warm or cold.

MAKES 16

Red Lentil Kofte with Pomegranate and Cilantro Salad

This recipe comes from the Zencefil café-restaurant in Istanbul, one of the most popular vegetarian restaurants in the city; it was given to me by my friend Ferda, the proprietor.

This is easy to prepare and a perfect light snack for summer days. Zencefil serves the little balls with a simple green salad.

Turkish red pepper paste can be bought from most Turkish and Middle Eastern shops. If you can't get hold of any, use tomato paste instead.

FOR THE KOFTE

- 2 **tablespoons olive oil**
- 1 **large red onion, finely chopped**
- 1 **tablespoon ground cumin**
- 1 **tablespoon Za'atar (page 249)**
- 1 **teaspoon sweet paprika**
- ½ **cup red lentils**
- 1 **tablespoon Pomegranate Molasses (page 249)**
- ⅔ **cup finely ground bulgur**
  sea salt and freshly ground pepper
- 3 **tablespoons finely chopped fresh cilantro**
- 1 **tablespoon mild red pepper paste or tomato paste**

FOR THE SALAD

  seeds from 1 pomegranate
- ½ **cup finely chopped fresh cilantro**

grated zest and juice
of 1 **small lemon**
- 3 **tablespoons olive oil**

To make the kofte

Heat the olive oil in a saucepan and sauté the red onion for 2–3 minutes. Add the cumin, za'atar and paprika, and cook for 2 minutes more. Stir in the lentils and then pour in the pomegranate molasses and 1⅓ cups water. Cover and simmer for 8–10 minutes, until the lentils are almost cooked. Add the bulgur, combine well and season. Tip the mixture into a bowl and let cool.

Once cool, stir in the cilantro and red pepper paste. Cover and refrigerate for 30 minutes to firm.

To make the salad

Combine all the ingredients in a bowl.

To serve

Shape the kofte mixture into mini balls and make a small indentation in the center of each. Spoon in the pomegranate and cilantro salad.

MAKES 30

White Butter Bean, Feta and Za'atar Spread

Fifty kilometers west of Damascus in Syria, perched 1,500 meters up the side of the Kalamun Mountains near the entrance to a gorge, lies the ancient village of Ma'alula. In fact, the name of the village means exactly that, "The Entrance."

The Syrians strive to keep its unique character. So, quite rightly, cars are banned from its streets. After the long, hot and dusty ride from the Syrian capital, my head still filled with the Hakawati's stories, we trudged wearily up a hill and staggered into a promising-looking café. I had visions of a bustling eatery, filled with locals tucking into some delicacy or other, imbibing cooling drinks made with lemons, or maybe yogurt with crushed ice.

The Al-Barakeh café sadly failed my aesthetic visions and the tables were empty of customers. We were greeted by the café owner who immediately offered us something to drink on the house – that's Syrian hospitality for you! I naturally felt obliged to order some food and more drinks, but an empty café does not inspire confidence and I must confess to wondering out loud what he might be able to offer.

Even in the tourist season, the owner explained, things were difficult, and this being October, there was little business. But he smiled one of those enigmatic smiles that Syrians seem to use for almost any occasion, and said that he would do his best.

It was this simple but wonderful dish, made with local goat cheese and served with freshly baked flat bread, that he brought to the table.

1 **cup dried butter or cannellini beans, soaked overnight in water to cover, drained and peeled**

sea salt and freshly ground pepper

1 **large head garlic, cut in half**

6 **tablespoons olive oil**

grated zest of 1 **lemon**

juice of ½ **small lemon**

5 **ounces crumbled feta**

2 **tablespoons finely chopped fresh mint**

½ **teaspoon cumin seeds, toasted and ground**

1 **teaspoon Za'atar (page 249)**

Preheat the oven to 400°F.

Bring a saucepan of water to boil and add the peeled beans. Reduce to a simmer and cook for 30 minutes until the beans are soft and mushy, then season. Cool, drain, then process to a rough puree.

Meanwhile, place the garlic on a small baking sheet, drizzle with a little olive oil and roast until soft, about 45 minutes. Cool, then squeeze the garlic out of its skin and add to the mashed beans. Stir half the olive oil into the bean mixture. Mix in the lemon zest and juice. Then add the feta, mint and cumin, stirring until you have a rough chunky puree, and season.

Place in a serving dish, drizzle with the rest of the olive oil and sprinkle with the za'atar. Serve with flat bread.

SERVES 8

*T*here was once a man called Hussein who saved up his money so that he might go on a pilgrimage to Mecca. When the time came, he had more money than was required to make the journey. He thought that he might give the excess to the poor, but what if he needed it upon his return?

After much deliberation he decided to leave the money with his neighbor, but not trusting him, he put the money in a bag and placed it in a jar, then filled the jar with oil and olives. Hussein went to the neighbor and asked him if he would look after the jar of olives while he traveled to Mecca, to which he agreed.

It so happened that while Hussein was away, his neighbor received some guests, and as was his way, he offered them raki, but was ashamed that he had no mezze to offer. Knowing that the olives would be easy to replace, he opened the jar, and there, at the bottom, he found the money in a bag. The neighbor was completely mystified, but put the coins in his pocket.

When Hussein returned from Mecca, he went to the neighbor and retrieved the olive jar, and to his horror, found that the money was gone! He angrily demanded to know where the money had gone.

"I can only but think," the neighbor said innocently, "that the coins have turned into olives."

That night, Hussein, a patient man, thought of a plan to get his money back.

From that day on, Hussein sought out his neighbor's company and they became even firmer friends than they had been before, and the son of Hussein became a friend of his neighbor's son.

Hussein purchased a monkey and kept it in a cage. He had also made an effigy of his neighbor, and the effigy was placed opposite the cage. Twice a day, for many months, food for the monkey was *placed on the effigy of the neighbor, and Hussein would open the cage saying, "Go to your father," and the monkey would sit on the effigy's shoulder and eat his food.*

One day, the neighbor's son was asked to Hussein's house so that he might play, and while he was there, he was invited to stay for a few days.

The neighbor came that evening to find out why his son had not returned, only to be told by Hussein that his son had changed into a monkey, and that becoming angry the monkey had had to be locked in a cage!

Hussein showed his neighbor the monkey, and upon seeing the neighbor, and recognizing him as the effigy, the monkey screamed for his food.

The next day the neighbor dragged Hussein before the courts to explain himself. Hussein brought the monkey along so that, God willing, they would see that he spoke the truth. The monkey was brought in and the cage opened. Hussein said, "Go to your father," and the monkey leapt onto the neighbor's shoulder. The neighbor protested that it was impossible for a child to be changed into a monkey, that it was against the laws of nature.

But Hussein stepped forward and declared that this was not true, that his neighbor had witnessed with his own eyes that money could be turned into olives, so why not a boy into a monkey?

Adapted from *Told in the Coffee House*, stories collected
in Istanbul by Cyrus Adler and Allan Ramsay (1898)

Jerusalem Artichoke Hummus Topped with Lamb and Sumac

This is another flavorful dish that I tried at the Al-Barakeh in Ma'alula, prepared along with a classic hummus. This version is made from Jerusalem artichokes instead of chickpeas, making the hummus lighter.

FOR THE LAMB

- 12 **ounces boneless lamb loin**
- 2 **teaspoons crushed sumac**
  sea salt and freshly ground pepper
- 2 **tablespoons olive oil**

FOR THE HUMMUS

- 1 **pound Jerusalem artichokes, peeled and chopped**
- ¼ **cup lemon juice**
- 1 **tablespoon cumin seeds, toasted and ground**
- 2 **tablespoons tahini**
- 2 **garlic cloves, minced**
- 6 **tablespoons olive oil**
  sea salt and freshly ground pepper

Preheat the oven to 400°F.

To cook the lamb

Place the lamb on a baking sheet, sprinkle with half the sumac, and season. Rub with the olive oil. Roast for 25–30 minutes, depending on how pink you like your lamb. Remove from the oven and allow to rest for 10 minutes.

To make the hummus

Place the Jerusalem artichokes in a saucepan and cover with cold water. Bring to the boil. Cook over medium heat for 12–15 minutes until soft. Drain and cool.

Puree the artichokes in a food processor. Add the lemon juice, cumin seeds, tahini and garlic. Pulsing the machine, gradually drizzle in the oil, and season.

To serve

Thinly slice the lamb. Spoon the hummus into a serving dish and arrange the lamb slices on top. Sprinkle with the remaining sumac.

SERVES 4

Lamb and Pistachio Kofte with Tahini and Pistachio Sauce

FOR THE SAUCE

- 1¾ cups unsalted pistachios
- ½ cup tahini
- juice of 2 lemons
- 3 garlic cloves, minced
- sea salt and freshly ground pepper

FOR THE KOFTE

- 14 ounces ground lamb
- 1 onion, grated
- 3 garlic cloves, minced
- ½ cup coarsely chopped pistachios
- ⅓ cup dried currants
- 2 tablespoons finely chopped fresh mint
- 2 tablespoons finely chopped fresh parsley
- ½ teaspoon sweet paprika
- ¼ teaspoon ground allspice
- ¼ teaspoon ground cinnamon
- sea salt and freshly ground black pepper
- ⅓ cup olive oil

To make the sauce

Lightly toast the pistachios in a dry skillet, stirring over medium heat until lightly golden. Allow to cool and put a few aside to use as garnish later. Finely grind the remainder in a food processor.

In a small bowl combine the tahini, lemon juice and garlic, and season. Then add 3–4 tablespoons of water so that the paste becomes thinner. Beat until you get the smooth consistency of heavy cream. Finally, add the ground pistachios and mix well. Refrigerate until needed.

To make the kofte

Combine all the ingredients except the oil, season, then shape into golf-ball-sized meatballs and slightly flatten. Heat the olive oil in a large nonstick pan. Fry the kofte, a few at a time, for 8–10 minutes, until golden brown and cooked through.

Serve with the tahini, pistachio sauce and reserved pistachios.

SERVES 6

Crunchy Red Swiss Chard Falafel

4 tablespoons olive oil

1 red onion, finely chopped

2 teaspoons ground cumin

¼ teaspoon ground allspice

1 pound red Swiss chard, well washed and roughly chopped

scant 1 cup milk

scant 1 cup chickpea flour

sea salt and freshly ground pepper

3 tablespoons cooked (canned) chickpeas

3 tablespoons lemon juice

vegetable oil for deep frying

ground turmeric for garnish

Tahini, Lemon and Sumac Sauce (page 25)

Heat 1 tablespoon of olive oil in a skillet and sauté the onion, cumin and allspice over medium heat for 3–4 minutes. Set aside in a bowl.

Fill a large saucepan with water and bring to the boil. Drop in the chard and blanch for 2 minutes. Drain immediately and, once they're cool enough to handle, squeeze dry.

In a medium nonstick saucepan, bring the milk to the boil, then reduce to a simmer. Little by little, whisk in the chickpea flour until you have a smooth paste. Keep the mixture moving to avoid lumps. Then season, add the remaining 3 tablespoons olive oil and cook over low heat for 8 minutes, stirring all the time with a wooden spoon. Like cream puff dough, the mixture will come away from the sides of the pan and become a ball as it is heated.

Cool the ball of paste, then mix in the sautéed onions, chickpeas, lemon juice and blanched chard. Using your hands, mold the mixture into golf-ball-sized balls and arrange on a baking sheet. Refrigerate for a couple of hours.

In a large saucepan, heat 2 inches of oil to 350°F. Carefully place the falafel into the oil and cook for 3–4 minutes, until golden brown. Remove with a slotted spoon and place on paper towels to drain.

Sprinkle with the turmeric. Serve with the tahini sauce.

SERVES 6

Crimson Beet Falafel

Serve these brilliant red-purple falafel with yogurt sprinkled with black sesame seeds.

4 tablespoons olive oil

1 large onion, finely chopped

2 teaspoons ground cumin

¼ teaspoon ground allspice

3 medium beets (14 ounces), scrubbed clean

scant 1 cup milk

scant 1 cup chickpea flour

sea salt and freshly ground pepper

3 tablespoons cooked chickpeas

2 tablespoons lemon juice

vegetable oil for deep frying

Heat 1 tablespoon of olive oil in a skillet and sauté the onion, cumin and allspice over medium heat for 3–4 minutes. Set aside in a bowl.

Cook the beets in plenty of water until three-quarters cooked (roughly 20 minutes). Drain, cool and peel the beets. Grate coarsely on a box grater (you might want to use rubber gloves to do this!).

In a medium nonstick pan, bring the milk to the boil, then reduce to a simmer. Little by little, whisk in the chickpea flour until you have a smooth paste. Keep the mixture moving to avoid lumps. Season, then add the remaining olive oil and cook over low heat for 8 minutes, stirring all the time with a wooden spoon. Like cream puff dough, as the mixture heats, it will come away from the sides of the pan and shape into a ball.

Cool the ball of paste, then mix in the sautéed onions, chickpeas, lemon juice and grated beets. Using your hands, mold the mixture into golf-ball-sized balls and arrange on a baking sheet. Refrigerate for a couple of hours.

In a large saucepan, heat 2 inches of oil to 350°F. Carefully place the falafel into the oil and cook for 3–4 minutes, until tinged golden brown. Remove with a slotted spoon and place on paper towels to drain.

SERVES 6

Three Tzatzikis: Beet, Zucchini and Spinach

FOR THE BEET TZATZIKI

- 4 medium beets, roasted (see page 58) and grated
- 2 garlic cloves, minced
- 3 tablespoons lemon juice
- 1½ cups Suzme (page 22)
  sea salt and freshly ground pepper
- 2–3 tablespoons olive oil
- 2 tablespoons finely chopped fresh parsley
- 2 tablespoons coarsely chopped walnuts

FOR THE ZUCCHINI TZATZIKI

- 3 tablespoons olive oil
- 4 small zucchini, finely sliced
- 2 tablespoons fresh thyme leaves
- 1½ cups Suzme (page 22)
- 3 tablespoons lemon juice
- 2 garlic cloves, minced
  sea salt and freshly ground pepper
- 2 tablespoons lightly toasted pine nuts

FOR THE SPINACH TZATZIKI

- 2–3 tablespoons olive oil
- 2 garlic cloves, minced
- 14 ounces fresh spinach, stems removed
- 1½ cups Suzme (page 22)
- 3 tablespoons lemon juice
  sea salt and freshly ground pepper
- 2 tablespoons sesame seeds, toasted

To make the beet tzatziki

Combine the beets, garlic, lemon juice and suzme, and season. Serve drizzled with the olive oil, and sprinkled with the parsley and walnuts.

To make the zucchini tzatziki

Heat half the olive oil in a nonstick pan. Gently sauté the zucchini and fresh thyme for 5–6 minutes, stirring constantly. Allow to cool.

Combine the cooled zucchini, suzme, lemon juice and garlic, and season. Serve, drizzled with the remaining olive oil and sprinkled with the pine nuts.

To make the spinach tzatziki

Heat the olive oil in a large pan and sauté the garlic. Add the spinach and cook for just a couple of minutes, until wilted. Drain very well, discarding any liquid. Let cool and squeeze with your hands until as dry as possible. Chop the spinach.

Combine the suzme, spinach and lemon juice, and season. Sprinkle with the sesame seeds.

Serve with pita bread, grilled meats, chicken kebabs or on their own as winter salads.

SERVES 6

Lamb and Spinach Yogurt Squares

FOR THE PASTRY

2½ cups self-rising flour

6 tablespoons cold unsalted butter, cubed

¼ teaspoon sea salt

⅓ cup yogurt

1 large egg yolk

1 tablespoon cumin seeds

FOR THE FILLING

12 ounces ground lamb

1 cup coarsely chopped pine nuts

1 Granny Smith apple, cored and grated

4 shallots, finely chopped

2 garlic cloves, minced

3 tablespoons finely chopped fresh cilantro

1 tablespoon Pomegranate Molasses (page 249)

½ teaspoon ground cinnamon

½ teaspoon ground nutmeg

½ teaspoon ground ginger
   sea salt and freshly ground pepper

8 ounces fresh spinach, stems removed

1 large egg yolk, beaten

To make the pastry

Pulse the flour, butter and salt to coarse crumbs in a food processor. Add the yogurt, egg yolk, 2 tablespoons cold water and cumin seeds, and pulse again. Turn the mixture into a bowl and knead into a smooth dough. Cover and refrigerate for 30 minutes.

To make the filling

Combine the lamb, pine nuts, apple, shallots, garlic, cilantro, pomegranate molasses, cinnamon, nutmeg and ginger in a bowl, and season to taste.

Meanwhile, bring a saucepan of water to boil and blanch the spinach for 1 minute. Drain immediately, let cool and squeeze dry. Chop coarsely, add to the meat mixture and thoroughly combine.

To cook the pastries

Preheat the oven to 400°F.

Let the dough stand at room temperature for 10 minutes. Divide the pastry into 3 pieces. Roll each piece to a ⅛-inch thickness, and cut into approximately 3-inch circles, using a cookie cutter or a cup.

Place a tablespoon of filling in the center of each circle, then pull up 4 edges of the pastry to create a square shape and pinch the corners closed. Repeat with the remaining dough and filling.

Mix the beaten egg yolk in a bowl with 2 tablespoons of water. Brush the pastries with the egg mixture and bake for 12–14 minutes, until golden brown.

MAKES 24

Creamy Feta and Caramelized Leek Börek

Börek is a Turkish pastry, made with either filo or yufka *pastry, then stuffed with various fillings, such as cheese, vegetable or meat. It can be a perfect snack, a light lunch or a main meal. From the days of my childhood I remember it as an eagerly anticipated afternoon snack, always accompanied by* ayran, *a Turkish yogurt drink.*

3 leeks, white and pale green parts, finely sliced

2 garlic cloves, minced

½ teaspoon sugar

2 tablespoons olive oil

1 tablespoon unsalted butter

¾ cup chicken stock

1 bay leaf

sea salt and freshly ground pepper

7 ounces feta, crumbled

2 tablespoons finely chopped fresh oregano

8 sheets of filo, thawed

melted butter, for brushing

2 tablespoons hemp, poppy and/or black sesame seeds

Preheat the oven to 400°F.

Sauté the leeks, garlic and sugar in the olive oil and butter in a skillet over medium heat for 4–5 minutes, stirring constantly. Add the stock and bay leaf, and season. Cook until the leeks are very tender, about 10 minutes. Remove the bay leaf and cool. Transfer the mixture to a bowl and combine with the cheese and oregano.

Spread a sheet of filo on the work surface, and cut lengthwise into thirds. Keep the remaining filo covered with a damp kitchen towel. Each strip will make 1 börek.

Brush a filo strip with melted butter and place a tablespoon of filling across the corner of one end. Fold this corner up and over to form a triangle and enclose the filling. Fold over again, and continue until you have a triangular pastry parcel. Repeat with remaining filo and filling.

Arrange the böreks on a baking sheet. Brush with more melted butter and sprinkle with the seeds. Bake for 20 minutes, until golden brown.

MAKES 24

Baba Ghanoush

This delicious baba ghanoush was served to me at the home of the Hakawati Abu Shadi. It is very similar to that which my own grandmother used to make; always a favorite, I never tire of it. Similarly to salad, this dish can be served on its own or with grilled meats and vegetables, kebabs or bread.

2 large eggplants

3 garlic cloves, minced

3 tablespoons tahini

juice of 2 large lemons

½ teaspoon ground cumin

¼ teaspoon sweet paprika

sea salt and freshly ground pepper

3 tablespoons finely chopped fresh parsley

1 tablespoon black sesame seeds

¼ teaspoon pink peppercorns, crushed

Place the eggplants directly on an open gas burner (or an electric burner) and, taking care, cook on medium heat for 10–12 minutes, turning occasionally, so that the eggplants are charred evenly. The skin will blacken and start blistering and the eggplants will soften, not to mention that your kitchen will be filled with a wonderful smell. Alternatively, you can bake them in the oven for 20 minutes at 425°F, but the flavor won't be quite the same. Place the eggplants in a thick plastic bag and allow them to sweat, which will make them easier to peel.

Peel and chop the eggplant flesh, discarding any uncooked pieces you might find. Place the chopped flesh into a sieve. Over a sink, press down gently to get rid of as much liquid as possible. Transfer the eggplant into a bowl and, using a fork, combine with the garlic, tahini, lemon juice, cumin and paprika. Or pulse in a food processor for a smoother mixture. Season.

Stir in the parsley. Serve sprinkled with black sesame seeds and crushed pink peppercorns.

SERVES 6

Damascene Walnut Tarator

Tarator is a Turkish-style sauce, based on nuts and herbs, with a hint of garlic and olive oil, a sort of pesto. Tarator sauces are often served as an accompaniment to fish and grilled vegetable dishes. They can be prepared using walnuts, pine nuts, almonds or hazelnuts. This is absolutely delicious, and is so easy it almost makes itself!

3 tablespoons finely chopped fresh parsley

1 cup finely chopped walnuts

2 tablespoons ground walnuts

2 tablespoons tahini

juice of 1 small lemon

2 garlic cloves, minced

½ teaspoon cayenne pepper

sea salt and freshly ground pepper

Put aside a little of the parsley for garnish. Combine all the ingredients to make a smooth paste. Season. Sprinkle with the reserved parsley and serve.

MAKES ABOUT 1⅓ CUPS

Pumpkin and Za'atar Hummus

1 pound sugar or pie pumpkin, peeled and seeds removed

¼ cup olive oil

sea salt and freshly ground pepper

3 garlic cloves, minced

3 tablespoons lemon juice

1 tablespoon Za'atar (page 249)

1 tablespoon ground cumin

1 tablespoon tahini, plus more for serving

2 tablespoons toasted pumpkin seeds

Preheat the oven to 400°F.

Cut the pumpkin into wedges. Place on a baking sheet, drizzle with the olive oil and season. Roast for about 45 minutes, until golden and soft. Remove from the oven and let cool. Pour off the oil.

In a bowl, roughly mash the cooled pumpkin with a fork. Add the garlic, lemon juice, za'atar, cumin and tahini, combine well and season. Place in a serving dish. Drizzle with a little tahini and sprinkle with toasted pumpkin seeds.

Serve with bread or crudités.

SERVES 6

Veal, Sour Cherry and Almond Stuffed Vine Leaves

FOR THE VINE LEAVES

50 fresh or preserved vine leaves

FOR THE STUFFING

2 tablespoons olive oil

1 medium shallot, finely chopped

14 ounces ground veal

½ cup long-grain rice

½ cup chicken stock

½ teaspoon ground cumin

sea salt and freshly ground pepper

¾ cup sliced almonds

⅔ cup dried sour cherries

3 tablespoons finely chopped fresh parsley

3 tablespoons finely chopped fresh mint

yogurt, for serving

To prepare the vine leaves

Select the 40 best leaves and set the remaining 10 leaves aside. Bring a saucepan of water to a boil. Add the leaves and cook 30 seconds for preserved leaves and 5 minutes for fresh. Drain and pat dry with paper towels.

To make the stuffing

Heat the olive oil in a deep skillet over medium heat and sauté the shallot for 3 minutes, until soft. Add the ground veal and cook until browned, about 5 minutes. Add the rice and chicken stock and simmer for about 10 minutes. Stir in the cumin, and season. When most of the liquid has been absorbed by the rice, mix in the almonds and sour cherries.

Remove from the heat, cover with a clean kitchen towel and a lid, and let stand for 10 minutes – it will continue to cook. This traditional method always produces a fluffy pilaf. Remove the towel and lid, and stir in the parsley and mint.

To cook the vine leaves

Lay out a leaf, shiny side down, and place a small amount of the veal mixture in the center – just enough to still be able to comfortably wrap the leaf around the mixture. Fold the bottom edge nearest you over the filling, then fold in the two sides and tightly roll away from you into a neat parcel.

Line the bottom of a medium-sized saucepan with 4 or 5 of the reserved leaves. Arrange the stuffed vine leaves, seam side down, in the saucepan, keeping them nice and tight in layers. Arrange the remaining leaves on top of the stuffed parcels. Add just enough water to cover. Weigh the parcels down with a plate to keep them in place. Simmer over low heat for 45–50 minutes.

Serve cool, with yogurt.

SERVES 6

Fennel and Feta Kofte with Walnut Tarator

Kofte are generally made from meat, but here is a version for vegetarians.

FOR THE WALNUT TARATOR

- 1 slice of bread, crust removed
- 1¾ cups walnuts
- 2 small garlic cloves, peeled
- 3 tablespoons coarsely chopped fresh parsley
- juice of 1 lemon
- ⅓ cup olive oil
- sea salt and freshly ground pepper

FOR THE KOFTE

- 1 large fennel bulb, finely shaved lengthwise into transparently thin strips
- 8 scallions, finely sliced
- 4 ounces feta, crumbled
- 3 large eggs
- 3 tablespoons finely chopped fresh parsley
- 3 tablespoons all-purpose flour, as needed
- 1 teaspoon fennel seeds, toasted
- 1 teaspoon baking powder
- ¼ cup olive oil
- coarsely chopped walnuts, for garnish

To make the walnut tarator

Soak the bread in a bowl of water. Remove, squeeze out any excess water and blend in a food processor with the walnuts, garlic, parsley and lemon juice, until the mixture forms a smooth puree. Add the olive oil, season and refrigerate until needed.

To make the kofte

Combine the fennel, scallions, feta, eggs, parsley, flour, fennel seeds and baking powder in a bowl. Add more flour, as needed, to make the mixture thick enough to shape. Season with black pepper. Roll the mixture into small patties. Heat the olive oil in a large frying pan. Add the kofte and cook for 2–3 minutes on each side, just a few at a time. Remove from the pan and place on paper towels to drain. Let cool.

Serve the kofte at room temperature, with the walnut tarator, sprinkled with the chopped walnuts.

SERVES 4

Beet Moutabel with Tahini and Toasted Orange Peel

A moutabel dip is a must on the Eastern Mediterranean mezze table. A traditional Syrian specialty, it was usually made with eggplant, but nowadays there are a variety of moutabels, such as beet, potato and zucchini.

Beet moutabel is not only delicious but a truly spectacular dish to look at because of its vibrant color.

5 **medium beets (about 1 pound), scrubbed clean**

2 **tablespoons olive oil**

sea salt and freshly ground pepper

finely chopped zest of 3 **oranges**

juice of ½ **lemon**

2 **tablespoons tahini**

2 **tablespoons Greek-style yogurt**

Preheat the oven to 400°F.

Arrange the beets in a roasting pan. Drizzle with olive oil, season and roast for about 1 hour, until tender. Let cool.

Meanwhile, scatter the orange zest in a small nonstick frying pan and toast over medium heat for about 1 minute. Let cool.

Peel the cooled beets. Grate half the beets on the finer holes of a box grater. Puree the other half in a food processor, but only roughly. This gives the moutabel more texture. Mix both beets in a bowl with the lemon, tahini and yogurt, and season.

Serve the moutabel topped with the toasted orange peel.

SERVES 6

Zucchini Moutabel

This is a specialty of Al Halabi, Four Seasons, in Damascus, a restaurant that to my mind produces the best regional food in Aleppo.

3 **medium zucchini**

¼ **cup olive oil**

juice of ½ **lemon**

2 **tablespoons tahini**

2 **tablespoons yogurt**

2 **tablespoons finely chopped fresh parsley**

Slice the zucchini lengthwise as thinly as you can manage, using a mandoline if you have one. Fry the zucchini in the olive oil in a skillet for about 1 minute on each side, until golden brown.

Transfer the zucchini onto paper towels to drain. Roughly mash them in a bowl with the lemon juice, tahini, yogurt and parsley.

SERVES 6

Sujuk Sausage Roll

Sujuk is a type of spicy sausage that is often eaten in the cooler months. I clearly remember my father making it just before Christmas – it was heavenly. His was made with pork, but in countries such as Syria and Turkey it is often prepared with lamb or beef.

This is another recipe that has endless variations, but here I have used the sujuk with puff pastry to create a type of Eastern Mediterranean sausage roll.

1 **pound ground lamb**

2 **garlic cloves, minced**

1 **teaspoon ground cumin**

1 **teaspoon sweet paprika**

1 **teaspoon dried mint**

1 **teaspoon dried oregano**

½ **teaspoon ground coriander**

½ **teaspoon hot red chili flakes**

¼ **teaspoon ground cinnamon**

¼ **teaspoon ground nutmeg**

sea salt and freshly ground pepper

1 **pound frozen puff pastry, thawed**

1 **large egg yolk, beaten**

3 **tablespoons hemp seeds**

Preheat the oven to 400°F.

Combine the lamb, garlic, cumin, paprika, mint, oregano, coriander, chili flakes, cinnamon and nutmeg, and season.

Roll the puff pastry into a square about ⅛ inch thick. Cut into long strips, roughly 3 inches wide. Arrange a long, thin layer of the sausage mixture down the center of each strip. For each strip, brush a long side of the pastry with water. Fold in half lengthwise so the edges meet, and press closed. Line a large baking sheet with parchment paper. Place the strips, seam sides down, on the sheet. Brush the tops with beaten egg and sprinkle with hemp seeds. Bake for 20–25 minutes, until golden brown. Cool slightly, then cut into 1-inch-thick slices and serve.

SERVES 8–10

Hummus

I wasn't going to include a hummus recipe in this book – there are just so many of them, and everyone knows how to make it, at least I thought so.

My hummus has always been deliciously light, silky and creamy (a nod to modesty here), laboriously made with chickpeas that have had their skins removed. An extremely tiresome job, but I believed it to be the best and only way to do it. Muhanad Jazier, chef at the Sednaya in Syria, showed me how wrong I was. So get out the bicarbonate of soda and a quantity of ice cubes, because you'll need them for this inspired method!

Muhanad showed me at least ten different types of hummus, all made from chickpeas, but all very distinctive. Beiruti, made with added yogurt, parsley and mint; Musabaha, a favorite in Jordan, incorporating whole chickpeas; and Damascus-style Kumuni, which contains no tahini but lots of cumin and olive oil.

So here is a variation that is very simple, yet produces a hummus of a light and silky texture, to be served with bread or crudités.

1 **pound dried chickpeas, soaked in cold water overnight**

1 **teaspoon baking soda**

4–5 **ice cubes**

¼ **cup tahini**

2 **garlic cloves, minced**

juice of 1 **lemon**

sea salt and freshly ground pepper

Drain the chickpeas, place them in a saucepan and cover with cold water. Add the baking soda and bring to the boil. Continue to simmer on low heat until the chickpeas are soft. Skim the foam from the top of the water from time to time.

Drain the chickpeas and reserve a few of them. Blend the remaining chickpeas in a food processor, dropping in the ice cubes one by one. This method produces a wonderfully smooth texture and turns the hummus almost white.

Transfer the blended chickpeas into a bowl, stir in the tahini (if you prefer a less nutty flavor, use less), garlic and lemon juice and season.

Serve topped with the reserved chickpeas.

SERVES 10

Toasted Citrus and Nasturtium Flower Aïoli

Aïoli is a classic Mediterranean sauce, made with olive oil, egg and garlic. Make sure you use top-quality fresh free-range eggs. This particular aïoli is flavored with fragrant toasted citrus zest and garnished with nasturtium flowers. It is perfect as an accompaniment to fish or vegetable dishes, or simply served with bread.

FOR THE TOASTED CITRUS

finely chopped zest of 1 **lemon**

finely chopped zest of 1 **lime**

finely chopped zest of 2 **oranges**

FOR THE AÏOLI

2 **large egg yolks**

½ **cup olive oil**

¼ **cup sunflower oil**

1 **teaspoon Dijon mustard**

1 **shallot, finely grated**

1 **garlic clove, minced**

1 **tablespoon lemon juice**

sea salt and freshly ground pepper

5–7 **orange or yellow nasturtium flowers**

Preheat the oven to 250°F.

To make the toasted citrus zest

Spread the lemon, lime and orange zests on a baking sheet lined with parchment paper. Bake for 15 minutes, until lightly toasted. Let cool.

To make the aïoli

Place the egg yolks in a food processor and turn on the machine. Slowly drizzle in the olive and sunflower oils until you have a thick creamy mixture.

Mix in the mustard, shallot, garlic, lemon juice and toasted citrus zests, and season. Serve topped with the nasturtium flowers.

MAKES ABOUT 1 CUP

Tahini and Black Sesame Bread Swirls

These moist, almost cakelike bread swirls are fun and easy to prepare at home and best eaten warm. I enjoyed them served with cake in the humble home of Abu Shadi; his wife had just made them for their lunch. Her version was rather spice-heavy, so I have slightly adjusted the cinnamon and completely removed the cloves and nutmeg she used.

3 tablespoons warm (105° to 115°F) water

1 teaspoon active dry yeast

1⅓ cups plus 1 tablespoon sugar

3¾ cups all-purpose flour

2 teaspoons ground cinnamon

2 teaspoons sea salt

2 tablespoons olive oil

½ cup tahini, plus more for topping

3 tablespoons black sesame seeds, plus more for topping

Mix the warm water and yeast in a small bowl. Add 1 tablespoon of sugar, stir and set aside for about 10 minutes until it becomes frothy.

In a separate bowl, combine the flour, cinnamon and salt. Add the yeast mixture, the olive oil and about 1 cup water, stirring to make a rough dough. Turn the dough out of the bowl and knead on a floured surface for 8–10 minutes, until smooth and elastic. Return the dough to the bowl, cover with plastic wrap and let rise 2 hours. Divide the dough into 2 balls, cover again and let stand for 10 minutes more.

Preheat the oven to 400°F. Line a large baking sheet with parchment paper. On a floured surface, roll a dough ball into a very thin 24-inch-diameter round, occasionally letting the dough rest for 2 minutes or so if it becomes too elastic to roll. Cut a 1-inch hole from the center of the round. Spread the dough with ¼ cup tahini, then sprinkle with ⅔ cup sugar and 1½ tablespoons sesame seeds. Using your fingers, roll up the dough from the hole toward the edge of the round, like rolling up a pants cuff, to create a ring of dough about 12 inches in diameter. An unusual technique, but this is how it's been done for centuries!

Cut the rope into 6 equal pieces. Coil each like a cinnamon roll, arrange on a baking sheet, then slightly flatten. Cover with plastic wrap. Spread each with a little additional tahini and sprinkle with sesame seeds. Repeat with the remaining ingredients. Bake for 25–30 minutes, until browned. Serve warm with hummus or jam.

MAKES 12

Avocado and Sumac Whip

This recipe is based on the principle of hummus preparation, only instead of chickpeas I have used velvety avocado, with a touch of nutty tahini and zesty sumac. While shooting the images for the book in Istanbul, I cooked a dinner for some Turkish friends and I prepared this very whip. They all loved it and declared it to be the Turkish version of guacamole, so you can best describe it like that, I guess! Serve with flat bread, lavash, or any crisp crackers – even tortilla chips.

2 ripe avocados

juice of 1 small lemon

¼ cup tahini, plus more for garnish

3 tablespoons olive oil

½ teaspoon crushed sumac

¼ teaspoon ground cinnamon

¼ teaspoon ground cumin

3 garlic cloves, minced

1 tablespoon black sesame seeds

Peel and cube the avocados, discarding the pits. Blend with the lemon juice in a food processor until smooth. Add the tahini, olive oil, sumac, cinnamon, cumin and garlic and mix together until it's the consistency of mayonnaise.

Sprinkle with the sesame seeds and a little more tahini, and serve.

SERVES 4

STARTERS

On the southern side of the Galata Bridge a great crowd of locals line up to buy a token to get them onto the Eminönü quayside for the twenty-minute trip across the Bosphorus from Europe into Asia.

On a wonderfully sunny afternoon, amid the smell of fried fish, I join the line, buy my token, and leap aboard the ferry just as the diesel engines roar and the gangplank is pulled in. The boat slips into the wide stream, the gulls scream and all manner of boat sirens give herald to our movement out into one of the world's busiest shipping lanes. I'm treated to a wondrous view of the Topkapi Palace and the minarets of the Blue Mosque, a sight that I have seen many times, but of which I will never tire. The fishy smoke follows us out across the water and slowly fades to be replaced by the salty tang of the sea.

The reason for my trip was to visit my favorite eateries, the Çiya restaurants of Kadýköy, three restaurants in the same street in the

fish market district that produce the most wonderful Anatolian cuisine. I was to meet with Musa Daðdeviren, the founder and owner.

Musa was born in Nizip in eastern Turkey, into a family of bakers and chefs. He came to Istanbul twenty years ago, with the belief that traditional Anatolian cooking needed to be resurrected before it became overwhelmed by the fast-food outlets that were springing up across Turkey's biggest city.

Over a traditional baba ghanoush I asked Musa what the name Çiya meant. He explained that it had three separate meanings: a wildflower from the mountains on the borders of Turkey and Syria; the sound of feet as they hit the floor during a traditional Georgian dance; and an old Turkish word for the sparkle of a fire. Each meaning is so wonderfully evocative and such a summing-up of what this cuisine has to offer, that Çiya could not be better named.

Jumbo Shrimp and Blood Orange Charmola Salad

This is a refreshingly light summer salad inspired by the Ottoman influence in North Africa. The blood orange season is short, but it can be made with any oranges. Charmola, a spice and herb paste, has many uses as a seasoning, and is often applied to seafood. There are many versions (mine has a base of sun-dried tomatoes), but cumin and cilantro seem to be the common thread.

12 **jumbo shrimp, shelled and deveined**

2 **large blood oranges, peeled and segmented**

8 **sun-dried tomatoes, soaked in warm water for 30 minutes, drained**

2 **large shallots, chopped**

1 **garlic clove, chopped**

¼ **cup olive oil**

1 **teaspoon ground cumin**

1 **teaspoon sweet paprika**

1-**inch piece of fresh ginger, peeled and finely chopped**

sea salt and freshly ground pepper

3 **tablespoons coarsely chopped cilantro**

Cook the shrimp in a large saucepan of boiling water for 3–4 minutes, until they turn opaque. Drain and cool. Place the shrimp and oranges in a large bowl.

Combine the sun-dried tomatoes, shallots, garlic, olive oil, cumin, paprika and ginger in a food processor and blend into a smooth paste. Add the paste to the shrimp and oranges. Toss together and season. Sprinkle with the cilantro and serve with crusty bread.

SERVES 4

Chickpea and Zucchini Kofte with Mulberry and Chive Flower Salad

Kofte is a meatball, often mixed with rice or bulgur; it can be fried, baked or grilled. Turkish cuisine has over 300 types of kofte. I was brought up with my mother's special kofte, which she made almost daily, and it was and still is my perfect fast food. This particular recipe is a vegetarian version and bulgur is used to bind the mixture, so using fine bulgur is very important. If you can't find fresh mulberries, which must be foraged, then use any dried berries or pomegranate seeds.

FOR THE KOFTE

- 7 tablespoons olive oil
- 1 medium red onion, peeled and finely grated
- 1 zucchini, grated
  sea salt and freshly ground pepper
- 1 teaspoon ground cumin
- 1 teaspoon hot paprika
- ½ teaspoon sweet paprika
- 1 cup dried chickpeas, soaked overnight in cold water
- ⅓ cup fine bulgur
- 2 tablespoons all-purpose flour, for dusting

To make the kofte

In a large saucepan, heat 3 tablespoons of olive oil and add the onion and zucchini. Season and cook for roughly 3 minutes, until tender, stirring constantly. Add the cumin and paprikas and stir well.

Drain the chickpeas, add to the onion and zucchini, then pour in 3½ cups of water and bring to a boil. Reduce to a simmer and cook for 15–20 minutes, until almost three-quarters of the liquid has been absorbed. Cool the mixture a little. Transfer to a food processor and pulse until crushed but not pureed. Stir in the bulgur, which will absorb the remaining liquid. Set aside for 15 minutes, then season.

FOR THE SALAD

- ⅓ cup fine bulgur
- 1 small red onion, thinly sliced
- 6–8 fresh mulberries or the seeds from 1 small pomegranate
- 2 tablespoons olive oil
- 1 tablespoon Pomegranate Molasses (page 249)
- 1 tablespoon lemon juice
- sea salt and freshly ground pepper
- ¼ cup finely chopped fresh chives
- 2 tablespoons toasted sliced almonds
- 6–8 fresh chive flowers

To make the salad

Combine the bulgur and 1 cup boiling water in a bowl and let stand until tender, about 10 minutes. Drain well in a fine wire sieve.

Combine the bulgur, onion, mulberries, olive oil, pomegranate molasses and lemon juice in a large bowl, and season. Mix in the chives, then sprinkle with the almonds and chive flowers. Set aside.

To cook the kofte

Using about 2 tablespoons of the kofte mixture for each, shape with your hands into balls. Dust with the flour. Heat the remaining oil in a large skillet over medium-high heat. Add the kofte and cook until lightly browned, about 1 minute on each side. Place on paper towels to drain. Serve warm with the salad.

SERVES 6

Sumac Braised Nettles Topped with Nigella Seeds

Nettles are the original free and wild food! Used mainly in soups, they are loaded with iron and exceptionally good to eat. Once blanched, they no longer sting. I remember my grandmother making wonderfully warming and vivid green nettle soup with a poached egg and a sprinkle of paprika.

If you don't plan on foraging for nettles, they can be found at large farmers' markets during the spring and summer. Because of the almost invisible tiny spikes on their leaves, they are also called stinging nettles. When handling fresh nettles, be sure to wear gloves, knowing that the offending little needles will disappear when cooked. This recipe also works well with spinach or watercress.

11 **ounces nettle leaves (see above)**

2¼ **cups hot water**

3 **tablespoons olive oil**

6 **scallions, finely sliced**

1 **garlic clove, minced**

¾ **cup long-grain rice**

sea salt and freshly ground pepper

½ **teaspoon crushed sumac**

1 **teaspoon nigella seeds, toasted**

4 **ounces feta**

Wearing gloves, place the nettles in a saucepan and add the hot water. Bring to a boil and cook for 1–2 minutes, until wilted. Drain, reserving 1 cup of the cooking water.

In a large saucepan gently heat the olive oil. Sauté the scallions and garlic for 2–3 minutes. Add the rice, stirring to ensure the grains are well coated with the oil. Finally, add the wilted nettles and the reserved cupful of water. Cover and simmer for about 17 minutes, until the rice is tender and all the liquid has been absorbed. Season, sprinkle with the sumac, stir well and serve topped with the toasted nigella seeds and a wedge of feta on the side.

SERVES 4

Poached Eggs with a Yogurt and Paprika Dressing

There are so many reasons why I miss my father, too many to recount. One thing that will remain with me always is the way he would whip up a delicious dish out of thin air, and how we would sit at the old wooden table outside our villa in the mountains and, with some local bread in hand, a tasty meal in front of us, we would talk, nothing special, just chitchat, and listen to the cowbells ringing in the distance. It was idyllic, something I will never forget.

This extremely simple dish was one of his favorites, but I make no excuse for including it. The Turkish love it and call it gilbir.

¼ cup white distilled vinegar

8 large eggs

1 garlic clove, minced (optional)

1⅔ cups yogurt

2 tablespoons unsalted butter

4 teaspoons sweet paprika

1 tablespoon finely chopped fresh mint

sea salt

Half fill a medium saucepan with salted water and add the vinegar. Bring to the boil and turn down the heat so that it is just gently simmering. The water must not be boiling vigorously.

One at a time, crack the eggs into a small bowl and gently slide them into the simmering water. Do not cook more than 2 at a time. If an egg seems to be going wrong and isn't keeping its shape, scoop it out with a spoon and start again. You'll need to cook the eggs for 3–4 minutes for a soft yolk, and at least 5 minutes for a hard yolk. Transfer the eggs with a slotted spoon to a large bowl of hot water to keep warm.

If desired, stir the garlic into the yogurt. Heat the butter until sizzling in a small skillet over low heat. Add and stir the paprika for 30 seconds (don't let it burn). For each serving, use the slotted spoon to transfer 2 eggs to a bowl. Top with the yogurt, drizzle with the paprika butter, and sprinkle with mint. Season and serve.

SERVES 4

Saffron and Lemon Soup
with Lobster

For this Eastern Mediterranean version of bouillabaisse, any chunky meaty fish will do. Monkfish works particularly well, but lobster makes it a very special dish indeed. Or you can use about 8 ounces peeled and deveined large shrimp – just add them to the soup during the last 5–6 minutes of cooking time.

1 **pound cooked lobster**

3 **pounds fish bones, for the stock**

2 **shallots, halved**

3 **celery ribs, chopped**

1 **carrot, chopped**

½ **small fennel bulb, chopped**

2 **bay leaves**

1 **garlic clove, peeled**

sea salt and freshly ground pepper

2 **ripe tomatoes, chopped**

¾ **cup dry white wine**

2 **ounces fine vermicelli, broken**

1 **teaspoon chopped fresh thyme**

pinch of **saffron**

4 **large egg yolks**

juice of 2 **lemons**

3 **tablespoons finely chopped fresh parsley**

Shell and break the lobster meat into bite-sized pieces. Set aside for later.

Place the fish bones, shallots, celery, carrot, fennel, bay leaves and garlic in a large saucepan and cover with water. Season, and bring to a boil. Reduce to a simmer and cook over low heat for 20 minutes. Strain the liquid into another saucepan and reserve as your soup stock. Discard the solids.

To the stock, add the tomatoes, white wine, vermicelli, thyme and saffron. Cook over low heat for 8–10 minutes, until the vermicelli is tender.

In a small bowl, whisk the egg yolks and lemon juice. Whisk about 1 cup of the hot soup into the yolks and lemon (not the other way round). Now stir this mixture into the soup. Briefly heat for 1–2 minutes to cook the yolks, but do not boil.

Ladle the soup into bowls, add the lobster pieces, and serve sprinkled with parsley.

SERVES 6

Pistachio and Sumac Crumbed Scallops with Pistachio Sauce

FOR THE SAUCE

- 1 **cup pistachios, coarsely chopped**
- ⅓ **cup coarsely chopped fresh parsley**
- juice of 1 **small lemon**
- 7 **tablespoons olive oil**
- **sea salt and freshly ground pepper**

FOR THE SCALLOPS

- a scant 1 **cup pistachios**
- 1 **tablespoon nigella seeds, toasted**
- 1 **teaspoon crushed sumac, finely ground in a spice grinder**
- 12 **large scallops**
- **melted butter, for brushing**
- 1 **tablespoon olive oil**

To make the sauce

Process the pistachios, parsley and lemon juice in a blender, drizzling in the olive oil a little at a time until you have a smooth, thick consistency, and season.

To cook the scallops

In a dry skillet, lightly toast the pistachios over medium-high heat. Let cool, place in a food processor and grind down to a powdery consistency. Pour into a bowl and combine with the nigella seeds and sumac. Brush each scallop with melted butter and roll in the pistachio mixture.

Heat the olive oil in a very large skillet or griddle over medium-high heat. Sear the scallops for 2–3 minutes on each side, until golden brown.

Arrange 3 scallops on each serving plate and drizzle with the pistachio sauce.

SERVES 4

Through a gap in the rocks, my eye fell on the strangest and most fantastic sight which man has ever seen: it was Damascus and its boundless desert, a few hundred feet below my path ... first the town, surrounded by its walls, a forest of minarets of all shapes, watered by the seven branches of its river, and streams without number, until the view is lost in a labyrinth of flower gardens and trees.

Alphonse de Lamartine (1833)

Until very recently I was madly in love with the great mystical city of Istanbul. I thought that no place could be so grand, nor so steeped in history, and that love has not diminished, but a new light has come into my life: Damascus.

Damascus, one of the greatest cities in history, was already old when Rome was founded. Its heritage seeps from every wall, permeating the fabric of the city and the very bones of the citizens, the friendliest people that I have ever had the pleasure to meet. Damascus's dilapidated grandeur is absolutely magical, oozing surreal emotions and passions in dreamlike splendor.

It is no exaggeration to say that visiting Damascus brings me a sense of renewal. It is like waking from a night's sleep a day younger, not older. All the words in the world cannot describe this place. You need to go there to feel its soul and energy, for it is for ever young.

Veal Sweetbreads in Cumin, Sumac and Mustard Crumb

I originally had this dish in a small café on the Asian side of the Bosphorus, where it was served with lamb sweetbreads. Personally I think veal sweetbreads are superior in taste and texture, so that's why I suggest you use them.

1½ **pounds veal sweetbreads, trimmed of excess fat**

1 **carrot, chopped**

1 **small onion, chopped**

1 **celery rib, chopped**

1⅓ **cups dried bread crumbs**

1 **teaspoon dry mustard**

1 **teaspoon crushed sumac**

1 **teaspoon ground cumin**

sea salt and freshly ground pepper

3 **tablespoons olive oil**

1 day in advance

Place the sweetbreads in a glass bowl and cover with cold water. Cover and refrigerate overnight.

On the day

Drain the sweetbreads and place them in a saucepan with the carrot, onion and celery. Cover with fresh water and bring to a boil. Reduce to a simmer and cook for 5 minutes. Drain, discarding the vegetables. Place the sweetbreads on a plate and peel off any excess membrane.

In a bowl, combine the bread crumbs, mustard, sumac and cumin, and season. Cut the sweetbreads into 1½-inch pieces, brush lightly with a little oil and roll them in the bread-crumb mixture until coated.

Heat the remaining oil in a nonstick skillet over medium-high heat. Lightly sauté the breaded sweetbreads on both sides to brown evenly, about 30 seconds per side.

Serve with Tomato, Pomegranate and Sumac Salad (page 126).

SERVES 4

Cheddar, Coriander and Chard Gözleme

Gözleme are a favorite Turkish street food, little pastries stuffed with meat, vegetables or cheese, then fried or cooked on a griddle. We used to make them at home with a yellow cheese, known as kashkaval. *It is a mild hard cheese, available in Turkish or Middle Eastern shops. Using a mild Cheddar or Gruyère as a substitute works well too.*

2 teaspoons olive oil

1 pound Swiss chard leaves, well rinsed and chopped

¼ cup chopped fresh cilantro

1 red onion, grated

1 long red fresh chile, seeded and finely chopped

2 garlic cloves, minced

1¾ cups (7 ounces) kashkaval or mild Cheddar, shredded

6 filo sheets, preferably thick filo, thawed

5 tablespoons clarified butter or ghee, melted

In a large skillet, heat the olive oil and sauté the chard, cilantro, onion, chile and garlic for 2–3 minutes, until the leaves have wilted. Remove from the heat, drain well, discarding the cooking juices. Cool in a glass bowl, then add the cheese.

Stack the filo sheets and cut through the stack into 13-inch squares. Discard the trimmings. Cut diagonally from corner to corner to cut each square into 2 triangles (12 triangles total). Cover with a damp kitchen towel.

Working with one triangle at a time, scatter some of the chard and cheese filling into the center and brush the sides with melted butter. Fold the points of the triangle so that they overlap and enclose the filling. Brush the tops with melted butter and arrange on a platter. Repeat to make 12 pastries.

Heat the remaining butter in a nonstick pan over medium heat. In batches, cook the gözleme in the butter for 2–3 minutes on each side, until golden brown.

Serve hot or cold.

MAKES 12

Almond and Roasted Garlic Soup with Toasted Coconut

This soup is best prepared with fresh green almonds straight from their velvety shells. Just like walnuts, almonds harden after harvest, so most of us are only familiar with the almond once it has turned brittle and brown. When still green, the almond is milky and very sweet. The season for fresh almonds is short, so if you're unable to get hold of any, use good-quality whole blanched almonds.

4 **whole garlic heads**

2 **tablespoons olive oil**

2 **tablespoons unsalted butter**

6 **shallots, thinly sliced**

2 **slices of brioche**

2 **cups (8 ounces) fresh green or blanched almonds**

1¾ **cups chicken stock**

sea salt and freshly ground pepper

½ **coconut, cracked, shelled, peeled and cut into large thin shreds**

Preheat the oven to 375°F.

Cut each garlic head in half and drizzle with 1 tablespoon of oil. Place in a small baking pan. Roast for about 40 minutes, until the garlic is soft. Set aside to cool, leaving the oven on.

In a saucepan, heat the butter and remaining oil over low heat and gently sauté the shallots for 8–10 minutes, until very tender but not browned. Remove from the heat. Squeeze the garlic out of its skin, like squeezing toothpaste from a tube. Stir the garlic into the sautéed shallots.

Cut the brioche into ½-inch cubes. Spread the brioche cubes and almonds on a baking sheet lined with parchment paper. Bake for 10 minutes, until they've just turned a light golden brown. Let cool. Meanwhile, bring the chicken stock to a boil in a large saucepan.

Put the cooled almonds and brioche in a food processor and process until finely ground. Add half the hot stock and process until you have a thick puree. Transfer the mixture to the remaining stock in the saucepan and stir well to combine. Add the shallots and garlic and again stir to combine. Simmer for a few more minutes, until you have a silky smooth, pureed soup. Season with salt and pepper.

Toast the coconut in a dry nonstick frying pan over medium-high heat, until golden. Let cool.

Serve the hot soup topped with the toasted coconut.

SERVES 6

Chilled Sweet Pea and Watercress Soup with Rose Petal Cream

FOR THE SOUP

- 4 **packed cups (5 ounces) watercress leaves**
- 1 **small onion, grated**
- 1 **quart water**
- 2 **cups shelled fresh peas**
- 2 **tablespoons finely chopped fresh parsley**
- 2 **tablespoons finely chopped fresh chervil**
- 2 **teaspoons finely chopped fresh thyme**
- **sea salt and freshly ground pepper**

FOR THE CREAM

- 2 **large unsprayed red or pink roses**
- ⅔ **cup heavy cream**
- **sea salt**
- pinch of **ground pink peppercorns**

To make the soup

Place the watercress and onion in a saucepan and add ⅔ cup of water. Bring to a boil. Reduce to a simmer and cook for just 1 minute. Now add the peas, parsley, chervil and thyme. Pour in the remaining water, season and bring back to a boil. Reduce the heat and simmer for 3 minutes.

To stop the soup overcooking, pour it straight into a heatproof bowl nestled in another bowl of ice cubes. Let cool completely. Puree in a food processor and pass through a fine sieve.

To make the cream

Pick off the rose petals from the stem and wash well. Set aside 6 petals for the garnish. Puree the remaining petals in a food processor.

Whisk the cream until thickened. Add the rose puree and season with salt and add a pinch of pink peppercorns.

To serve

Serve the soup with a dollop of the rose petal cream and scattered with the reserved rose petals.

SERVES 6

Yogurt and Oregano Pesto Soup with Oregano Flowers

Eaten throughout Turkey, this soup is especially popular in Anatolia and is also found in Syria. It is served hot, most often flavored with mint, cornstarch being used to stabilize the yogurt. Here I have used oregano instead of mint. As it is a seasonal soup, made with fresh oregano, I love using the flowers of the plant too!

FOR THE OREGANO PESTO

- 24 sprigs of fresh oregano, leaves and flowers
- 2 garlic cloves, minced
- 1 cup pine nuts
- 1/3 cup olive oil
- 3 tablespoons freshly grated Parmesan

FOR THE SOUP

- 1 tablespoon olive oil
- 1 celery rib, chopped
- 1 carrot, chopped
- 1/2 onion, chopped
- 3 sprigs of fresh thyme
- 3 sprigs of fresh oregano
- 1 bay leaf
- sea salt and freshly ground pepper
- 5 cups chicken stock
- 2 tablespoons Arborio rice
- 1 tablespoon cornstarch
- 1 pound Greek-style yogurt, drained in a cheesecloth-lined wire sieve for 1 hour
- 2 large egg yolks
- 1 teaspoon hot red chili flakes
- 1/2 cup cooked chickpeas

To make the oregano pesto

Set aside some of the oregano flowers for the garnish. Using a mortar and pestle, make a chunky paste with the oregano and garlic (or use a food processor if you prefer a smoother paste), then add the pine nuts and grind. Gradually add the olive oil. Stir in the Parmesan. If you would like your pesto to have a little thinner consistency, add a touch more olive oil. Refrigerate until needed.

To make the soup

In a large saucepan, heat the olive oil over medium heat and cook the celery, carrot and onion for 2–3 minutes. Add the thyme, oregano and bay leaf, and season. Now pour in the stock. Simmer gently for 15 minutes, then strain into another saucepan and discard the solids. Add the rice to the strained stock and cook for 30 minutes, until tender.

Spoon a tablespoon of cornstarch into a small bowl, add a little of the soup and mix well. Pour the yogurt into a separate bowl and add 3 tablespoons of soup, beat for a moment, then add the egg yolks and the cornstarch mixture. Stir well.

Pour the yogurt mixture into the soup and cook over medium-low heat, just to a simmer and until lightly thickened. Take care not to let it boil, as this will curdle the yogurt.

Add the chili flakes, and season with salt.

To serve

Serve hot in large deep dishes. Put a small handful of chickpeas in the middle, top with a spoonful of the oregano pesto, and finish with the fresh oregano flowers.

SERVES 6–8

Egg and Lemon Soup with Fresh Crab and Lemon Balm

Nothing speaks more of the Eastern Mediterranean than the lemon, and personally speaking, I will add lemon juice to almost any fish or soup dish. Eggs and lemon, or terbiye, *can also be cooked with rice rather than orzo. Adding lemon balm gives an extra lemony flavor.*

1 quart light chicken stock (made from unbrowned bones)

6 tablespoons orzo

4 large egg yolks

grated zest and juice of 1 large lemon

4 ounces arugula, coarsely chopped

sea salt and freshly ground pepper

10 ounces cooked crabmeat, picked over for shells and cartilage

½ teaspoon crushed sumac

4 sprigs of fresh lemon balm, leaves only, finely chopped

Bring the stock to a boil in a large saucepan over medium heat. Reduce the heat, add the orzo and simmer for 25 minutes, until the orzo is very tender.

Combine the egg yolks, lemon zest and juice in a bowl. Mix in about ½ cup of the hot stock, then stir into the saucepan. Add the arugula and season. Simmer for 3–4 minutes more, until the arugula is thoroughly wilted. Finally, add the crabmeat and cook for a minute longer, until heated through.

Remove from the heat and serve topped with a sprinkle of sumac and chopped lemon balm.

SERVES 6–8

BÖREKS, PILAFS & SALADS

Börek

Börek is quintessentially Turkish! Some of the best böreks in the world are served from stalls on the street corners of Turkey and Syria. They are light, fluffy, crispy pastries filled with whatever the season has brought to the kitchen. Usually made with either filo or Turkish yufka, they can also be prepared with yogurt-based dough or puff pastry.

Sweet Potato and Scallion Börek

2 large sweet potatoes, peeled and cubed

1 tablespoon unsalted butter

6 scallions, finely sliced

½ teaspoon sweet paprika

2½ teaspoons nigella seeds

4 sheets of filo, thawed
melted butter, for brushing

1 large egg yolk, beaten

Preheat the oven to 375°F.

Place the sweet potatoes in a saucepan of cold water and bring to a boil. Reduce to a simmer for 12–15 minutes, until the potatoes are soft. Drain and coarsely mash the sweet potatoes – you don't want them to be too smooth.

Heat the butter in a deep saucepan and sauté the scallions for 1 minute. Add the warm sweet potatoes, paprika and 1½ teaspoons of the nigella seeds. Combine well. Let cool.

Place a sheet of filo pastry on your work surface and brush with melted butter, then immediately place another sheet of filo on top of the first. (Filo can dry quickly, so keep the pastry that you are not using under a damp cloth.) Spoon half the potato mixture along the bottom edge of the stacked filo. Roll away from you to form a thin sausage and tuck the ends in. Repeat the process with the remaining filo and filling.

Arrange the 2 böreks on a baking sheet, brush with the beaten egg and sprinkle with the remaining nigella seeds. Bake for 12–15 minutes, until golden. Cut up and serve warm. Simple and delicious!

SERVES 6

Lentil and Swiss Chard Börek

FOR THE PASTRY

- 2½ cups self-rising flour
- 6 tablespoons cold butter, cubed
- 6 tablespoons crème fraîche or sour cream
- 1 egg yolk
- ¼ teaspoon sea salt
- all-purpose flour, for dusting

- 1 egg yolk, for brushing
- 1 tablespoon white sesame seeds

FOR THE FILLING

- ½ cup green lentils
- 2 tablespoons olive oil
- 6 scallions, finely sliced
- 7 ounces Swiss chard leaves, chopped
- sea salt and freshly ground pepper

Preheat the oven to 375°F.

To make the pastry

Pulse the flour and butter in a food processor until you have coarse crumbs. Add the crème fraîche, ¼ cup water, egg yolk and salt and pulse to get a soft, smooth dough. Cover and refrigerate for 30 minutes.

To make the filling

Place the lentils in a small saucepan and add cold water to cover. Bring to a boil over high heat. Reduce the heat to a simmer and cook about 30 minutes, until tender. Drain and let cool.

Heat the oil in a large skillet and sauté the scallions for 2 minutes. Add the Swiss chard and cook for 2 minutes more, until wilted. Add the lentils. Season and let cool.

To cook the börek

Remove the dough from the refrigerator and let stand at room temperature for 5 minutes. Dust a work surface with flour and roll out the dough to roughly 16 inches square, about ⅛ inch thick. Cut the pastry into 5 horizontal strips, then cut in the opposite direction to make 25 equal squares.

Make an egg wash by beating the egg yolk with ½ teaspoon water. Lightly brush the edges of each square with the egg wash. Place a small amount of the filling in the center of each square. For each square, lift one corner and fold it to the diagonally opposite corner. Seal the edges to encase the filling so that you have triangular-shaped parcels. Brush the top of each parcel with a little more egg wash, then arrange the parcels on a baking sheet and sprinkle with the sesame seeds. Bake for about 30 minutes, until golden brown.

MAKES 25

Wild Greens and Feta Börek

This börek is built with an unusual technique of brushing the layers with a custard, making it especially rich. Use any wild greens that are available, or use spinach or watercress instead.

2 tablespoons olive oil, plus more for the dish

10 ounces arugula

7 ounces nettles (see page 76)

7 ounces feta, crumbled

½ teaspoon ground black pepper

½ teaspoon cayenne pepper

2 large eggs

1 cup milk

6 tablespoons unsalted butter, melted

10 sheets of thin filo, thawed

2 tablespoons nigella seeds, toasted

8 × 8-inch square baking pan

Preheat the oven to 400°F.

Heat the olive oil in a saucepan and sauté the arugula and nettles (don't forget to wear gloves) for 2 minutes, until just wilted. Let cool. With your hands, thoroughly squeeze dry the greens and place them in a large bowl. Add the feta and the black and cayenne peppers, and combine.

Stack the filo. Cut through the top sheet to make twenty 8-inch squares. Discard the trimmings.

In another bowl, whisk the eggs, then whisk in the milk and melted butter. Oil the baking pan. Line with a sheet of filo, brush it generously with the egg mixture, then top with another sheet. Repeat the process until you have used half the filo sheets.

Spoon in the greens and feta mixture and top with the remaining filo sheets as before, brushing with the egg mixture between each layer. Pour any remaining egg mixture over the final layer and sprinkle with nigella seeds.

Bake about 35 minutes, or until golden brown. Let cool.

Cut into diamond shapes and serve.

SERVES 8

Pilaf

The pilaf is the emperor of rice dishes: exquisite, seductive, light, velvety and simply irresistible! Traditionally the best rice to use is baldo, a starchy medium-grain rice, but Arborio or basmati rice can be substituted; this modern and light pilaf uses wild rice.

Wild Rice Pilaf with Spinach and Fava Beans

1 **pound fresh fava beans, in their pods**

1 **cup wild rice, soaked in cold water for 12 hours**

2 **tablespoons unsalted butter**

1 **onion, finely chopped**

sea salt and freshly ground pepper

1 **quart vegetable stock**

14 **ounces spinach leaves, chopped**

½ **cup pine nuts, lightly toasted**

3 **tablespoons coarsely chopped fresh parsley**

zest of 1 **lemon**

TO SERVE

1 **cup yogurt**

2 **tablespoons olive oil**

sweet paprika, for garnish

Remove the beans from the pods and drop them into a saucepan of boiling water. Simmer for 3–5 minutes, then drain and rinse under cold water. Let cool. Remove the outer skins.

Drain the rice. (I presoak it, as this makes it quicker to cook.) Heat the butter in a saucepan over medium heat and sauté the onion for 3–4 minutes. Add the rice and cook for 2 minutes, stirring all the time. Season and add the vegetable stock. Bring to a boil, cover and simmer over low heat for 20–35 minutes, until the rice is almost tender. Remove from the heat, cover and let stand for about 15 minutes, until the rice is tender. Stir in the spinach, fava beans, pine nuts, parsley and lemon zest. Drain if needed.

To serve

Fluff the rice with a fork and serve with a dollop of yogurt, a drizzle of olive oil and a sprinkle of sweet paprika.

SERVES 4

Pilaf with Vermicelli, Chickpeas, Apricots and Pistachios

This is street food, Turkish-style. This dish can be found in the markets of Istanbul, sold as a hot lunch, often topped with freshly boiled chicken breast. Be sure to let the rice stand for at least 15 minutes to finish cooking before serving.

2 **shallots, sliced**

2 **tablespoons clarified butter or ghee**

3 **ounces vermicelli pasta, broken into 1-inch lengths**

1½ **cups baldo or Arborio rice**

1 **cup cooked chickpeas**

½ **cup chopped dried apricots**

2 **cups vegetable stock**

sea salt and freshly ground pepper

½ **cup coarsely chopped pistachios**

In a saucepan, sauté the shallots in the butter for 2 minutes over medium heat. Add the vermicelli and, continually stirring, cook until golden, keeping an eye on it because this happens pretty quickly. Add the rice, chickpeas and apricots, making sure the rice is well coated with the butter. Pour in the stock and bring to a boil. Reduce to a simmer, season and cover with a lid. Cook over low heat for 15–20 minutes, without stirring. Have a look from time to time, and add water if needed.

When the rice is tender, add the pistachios and turn off the heat. Cover the saucepan with a clean towel and replace the lid. Let stand for 15–20 minutes – this will allow the rice to cook further while becoming lovely and fluffy.

SERVES 4

Kadirga Pilaf with Pistachios, Almonds and Currants, Topped with Béchamel Sauce

This elegant pilaf is an extremely old recipe, and another favorite of the Ottomans that I reworked for today's kitchen.

FOR THE PILAF

- 2 **tablespoons unsalted butter**
- ¾ **cup dried currants**
- 2 **shallots, grated**
- 2 **garlic cloves, minced**
- 1¼ **cups baldo or Arborio rice**
- 1¾ **cups chicken stock**
- ¾ **cup coarsely chopped pistachios**
- ½ **cup coarsely chopped blanched almonds**
- 2 **tablespoons finely chopped fresh oregano**
- 2 **tablespoons finely chopped fresh parsley**

FOR THE BÉCHAMEL SAUCE

- 2 **tablespoons butter**
- 2 **tablespoons all-purpose flour**
- 1 **cup milk**
- ½ **teaspoon ground nutmeg**
  sea salt and freshly ground pepper
- 1 **cup (4 ounces) shredded Gruyère**

Preheat the oven to 400°F.

To make the pilaf

Melt the butter in an ovenproof casserole dish over medium heat. Sauté the currants, shallots and garlic in the butter for 1 minute, then add the rice, coating thoroughly. Pour in the stock, then cover and cook for about 15 minutes over very low heat, until the rice is tender. Remove from the heat, add the pistachios, almonds, oregano and parsley, and combine well.

To make the béchamel sauce

Heat the butter in a small saucepan over medium-low heat until melted. Add the flour, stirring all the time until it becomes a smooth paste. Whisk in the milk, adding a little at a time, then add the nutmeg, and season. Simmer over low heat for 5 minutes, taking care not to let the sauce come to a full boil. Finally, add the cheese and stir until it has all melted into the sauce.

Pour the sauce over the pilaf and transfer to the oven for 5 minutes, until the top is golden.

Serve hot.

SERVES 4–6

the parcel into the skillet. Cook over medium-low heat for 2–3 minutes, until the pastry is golden and crispy. Place the rimless baking sheet on top of the skillet, hold together and smartly turn over, so the pastry is on the sheet. Slide the pastry back into the skillet and cook on the other side for 2–3 minutes.

Place the skillet in the oven and bake until the pilaf is heated through, about 6 minutes.

Slide the pastry onto a platter. Cut into wedges and serve hot.

SERVES 4

Salads

The spring and summer bring to the markets of the Eastern Mediterranean the most wonderful displays of salad ingredients. Fresh tomatoes that have never been anywhere near a hothouse, for example, are an absolute delight, their flavor dancing on the taste buds. The wonderful little gems that are the fruits of the pomegranate, the mouthwatering cucumber, the crunchy nuts and velvety beans, the oranges, the artichokes, the avocados – all in plump abundance. There is only one rule when preparing salads: always use the freshest ingredients.

Purslane, Tomato and Avocado Salad

This is a typical salad from the Gaziantep region, where purslane is known as pirpirim. *It is often served as an accompaniment to kebabs. Purslane is among the most common greens in spring and summertime in the Eastern Mediterranean. It is known as an edible plant and weed, and its taste is not dissimilar to watercress or spinach, so you can substitute either.*

6	cups coarsely torn fresh purslane
¼	cup finely chopped fresh flat-leaf parsley
3	ripe plum tomatoes, cubed
1	avocado, pitted, peeled and cut into small cubes
1	green pepper, seeded and finely chopped
1	red onion, cut into thin rings
juice of ½	small lemon
1	teaspoon Pomegranate Molasses (page 249)
1	teaspoon crushed sumac
1	teaspoon sweet paprika
2–3	tablespoons olive oil
	sea salt and freshly ground pepper

Combine the purslane, parsley, tomatoes, avocado, green pepper and red onion in a large bowl. In a separate bowl, combine the lemon juice, pomegranate molasses, sumac and paprika and whisk in the olive oil. Drizzle over the salad, and season. Serve at once.

SERVES 6

Father's Smoked Eggplant and Hibiscus Salt Salad

The smell of charred eggplants – nutty, smoky and caramelized – is seductive, and that's what makes this salad what it is. Dried hibiscus flowers are used quite a bit in traditional Turkish cuisine and are renowned for their medicinal properties. Here I have made my own hibiscus salt, using dried hibiscus flowers (available at Mediterranean and Latino groceries). The salt is also delicious with fish.

FOR THE HIBISCUS SALT

- 1 **tablespoon dried hibiscus flowers**
- 1 **tablespoon flaky sea salt, such as Maldon or** *fleur de sel*

FOR THE SALAD

- 2 **medium eggplants**
- 3 **sweet red peppers**
- 1 **ripe tomato, finely chopped**
- juice of 2 **lemons**
- 2 **tablespoons olive oil**
- 3 **garlic cloves, minced**
- 1 **teaspoon ground cumin**
  sea salt and freshly ground pepper
- 3 **tablespoons chopped fresh parsley**
- 3 **tablespoons skinned and chopped hazelnuts**

2 days in advance

Place the dried hibiscus flowers in a food processor and pulse to a rough powder. Place in a small bowl, add the salt, mix well and cover. Allow to infuse for 2 days before using. You'll only need a small quantity for this recipe, but you can keep it in a container for up to a month.

On the day

Place the eggplants directly onto a stove burner over medium heat, gas or electric, and keep turning until they are evenly blistered, blackened and soft. This will take 10–15 minutes. Once cooked, place the eggplants in a sturdy plastic bag and let cool – this will make them easier to peel. Peel the eggplants and discard the skin. Slice the flesh into very thin strips and place into a large bowl. Any bits of the eggplants that have not cooked should be discarded.

Repeat the blackening process for the peppers, also cutting them into thin strips once cooled and peeled, discarding the seeds. Add to the eggplant.

Add the tomato, lemon juice, olive oil, garlic and cumin, and season to taste.

Sprinkle with the parsley, hazelnuts and the hibiscus salt.

SERVES 4

Chicken Liver, Potato and Aleppo Pepper Salad

2 large baking potatoes, peeled

4 tablespoons olive oil

14 ounces chicken livers, trimmed

sea salt and freshly ground pepper

8 scallions, finely sliced

3 tablespoons fresh parsley leaves, unchopped

grated zest and juice of 1 small lemon

1 teaspoon crushed Aleppo pepper

2 hard-boiled eggs, quartered

Boil the potatoes until just cooked. Drain and let cool. Cut them into cubes.

Meanwhile, heat 1 tablespoon of the oil in a skillet over medium heat and sauté the chicken livers until cooked and golden brown, about 5 minutes. Season, cool, then roughly chop.

Place the diced potatoes, chicken livers, scallions, parsley and lemon zest and juice in a large bowl and toss gently to combine. Season, drizzle with the remaining olive oil and sprinkle with the Aleppo pepper. Serve with the egg quarters arranged on top.

SERVES 4–6

Tomato, Pomegranate and Sumac Salad with a Pomegranate Dressing

The combination of sumac and tomato was made in heaven. This salad is best in the summertime when you can buy tomatoes that have not been grown in a greenhouse, when they are sweet and delicious. I discovered this salad on my very first trip to Istanbul. It is very common and the simplest of salads, but I was blown away by it!

6	ripe plum tomatoes
seeds of 1	pomegranate
¼	cup olive oil
2	tablespoons Pomegranate Molasses (page 249)
1	teaspoon crushed sumac
½	teaspoon ground cumin
	sea salt and freshly ground pepper

Slice the tomatoes and place in a large bowl. Add the pomegranate seeds and combine. Mix together the olive oil, pomegranate molasses, sumac and cumin in a bowl. Pour over the salad, season with salt and pepper and gently toss. Serve at once.

SERVES 6

Artichoke, Goat Cheese and Dried Cherry Salad

juice of 2 **lemons**

8 **baby artichokes**

1 **cup shelled fava beans**

1 **cup shelled fresh peas**

7 **ounces goat cheese, crumbled**

2 **tablespoons olive oil**

¼ **cup shelled pistachios**

2 **tablespoons Pomegranate Molasses (page 249)**

2 **tablespoons dried cherries**

½ **teaspoon ground cumin**

grated zest of 1 **orange**

sea salt and freshly ground pepper

Have ready a bowl of water with half the lemon juice in it – save the rest for later. Cut the top inch from the artichokes. Remove the outer leaves to reach the tender, light green heart. Using a small knife, pare off the dark green skin from the base of each heart and cut ½ inch from the top. Then drop the artichoke hearts into the lemon water to avoid discoloration. Bring a small saucepan of water to a boil. Add the artichokes, flat side down, cover and simmer for 15–20 minutes, until the artichokes are tender. Add the fava beans to the pan with the peas in the last 5 minutes of cooking. Remove from the heat and drain. Let cool and cut the artichokes into small wedges. If the fava bean skins are tough, peel them.

Gently toss the artichokes, beans and peas with the goat cheese, remaining lemon juice, olive oil, pistachios, pomegranate molasses, cherries and cumin. Sprinkle with the orange zest, and season with salt and pepper. Serve at once.

SERVES 4

MEAT &
POULTRY

One evening an old farmer went to his well to draw water for his animals. A strange light appeared to come from deep inside, so he peered into the darkness and there, at the bottom, was the moon.

The farmer knew his duty; he must rescue the moon and place it back in the firmament. Finding a rope, he tied a hook to one end and dropped it down into the well, where it caught upon a rock. The old man pulled and pulled, strained and puffed, and tugged, eventually the rope broke and he fell on his back.

Staring up into the heavens, he saw the moon high in the sky. He cried out in joy, "Praise be and honor to Allah, I have returned the moon to where it belongs."

Adapted from *Told in the Coffee House*, stories collected
in Istanbul by Cyrus Adler and Allan Ramsay (1898)

Lamb and Pistachio Kebabs

The best place in the world to eat kebabs is Istanbul, and the Beyti restaurant in Florya, founded more than sixty years ago, is the place to go to try them.

This is a recipe for a typical style of kebab from the Gaziantep region, where pistachios are used widely in all areas of cooking. The secret of this kebab is not to buy ground meat but to either finely chop the lamb or grind it yourself.

2 pounds boneless lamb shoulder

3 tablespoons finely chopped fresh parsley

2 red onions, finely grated

2 garlic cloves, minced

1½ cups chopped pistachios

1 teaspoon ground cumin

½ teaspoon sweet paprika

½ teaspoon freshly ground black pepper

¼ teaspoon ground cloves

¼ teaspoon ground coriander

¼ teaspoon ground cardamom

pinch of ground cinnamon

pinch of freshly grated nutmeg

2 tablespoons olive oil, for brushing

Trim the lamb of excess surface fat and cut into 1-inch cubes. Freeze on a baking sheet until very firm, about 1 hour. In batches, process the lamb in a food processor with the chopping blade until very finely chopped.

Combine the lamb and the remaining ingredients, except for the olive oil. Knead the mixture for at least 10 minutes, until smooth and well combined.

Split the mixture into 12 equal amounts, and shape into ovals. Refrigerate for 30 minutes.

Brush the meat ovals with the olive oil. Heat a ridged grill pan or griddle over medium heat. Cook the kebabs for 12–15 minutes, turning occasionally, until golden brown.

Serve with Tomato, Pomegranate and Sumac Salad (page 126).

SERVES 6

Sumac and Chili Spiced Rack of Lamb with Sweet Pomegranate Sauce

FOR THE LAMB

- 3 tablespoons crushed sumac
- 1½ teaspoons sea salt
- 1 teaspoon ground cumin
- ½ teaspoon hot red chili flakes
- 4 lamb racks, 3 ribs each, French-trimmed
- ¼ cup olive oil

FOR THE SAUCE

- ⅔ cup Pomegranate Molasses (page 249)
- 3 tablespoons grenadine
- 3 tablespoons honey

1 hour in advance

Combine the sumac, salt, cumin and chili flakes in a bowl, and season. Arrange the lamb racks in a roasting pan and rub all over with the sumac mix. Drizzle with olive oil and refrigerate for 1 hour.

Preheat the oven to 425°F.

To make the sauce

Place pomegranate molasses, grenadine, honey and 3 tablespoons water in a small saucepan. Bring to a boil, then reduce to a simmer. Cook for 10–12 minutes, until you have a syrupy consistency and have reduced the liquid by half.

To cook the lamb

Place the lamb racks in the oven and roast for 20 minutes, until an instant-read thermometer inserted in the center of a rack reads 125°F for medium-rare lamb. Let stand at room temperature for 10 minutes. Slice into chops and drizzle with the pomegranate sauce.

Serve with Baba Ghanoush (page 53).

SERVES 4

Partridge Dolma

Dolma is the Turkish method for stuffing anything, one of the most iconic and ancient methods in Eastern Mediterranean cuisine. The restaurant at the Ciragan Palace has a reputation for serving food with Ottoman influences. The chefs there create Ottoman dishes for the modern day, and this stuffed partridge dish is no different. It also works well with poussin.

FOR THE PARTRIDGES

- 4 **9-ounce partridges**
- **sea salt and freshly ground pepper**
- ¼ **cup olive oil**
- 2 **tablespoons unsalted butter**
- 6 **small shallots, peeled**
- 6 **garlic cloves, peeled**
- 2 **bay leaves**
- 6 **fresh thyme sprigs**
- 8 **prunes, pitted and chopped**
- 4 **dried apricots, chopped**
- ⅔ **cup chicken stock**

FOR THE STUFFING

- 1 **pound ground chicken**
- 6 **dried apricots, finely chopped**
- ¾ **cup coarsely chopped pistachios**
- 1 **teaspoon finely chopped thyme**
- **sea salt and freshly ground pepper**

Preheat the oven to 400°F.

To prepare the partridges

Bone the partridges, keeping the drumsticks and wings intact, or ask your butcher to do this. Lay each bird out flat and skin-down, and season.

To make the stuffing

Combine the stuffing ingredients, and season. Divide the stuffing among the birds, then roll them into a sausage shape to enclose the filling. Using kitchen string, tie securely.

To cook the partridges

Heat the olive oil and butter in a metal roasting pan over medium heat. Add the partridges and brown for 3–4 minutes on each side. Add the shallots, garlic, bay leaves, thyme, prunes and apricots and then the stock. Cover the dish with foil and roast for 30 minutes, until the partridges are just pink when pierced with the tip of a knife. Remove the foil and cook to lightly brown the partridges, about 10 minutes more. Let stand 5 minutes.

To serve

Remove the strings and cut each partridge crosswise into thick slices. Transfer each partridge to a dinner plate, and spoon the mixture in the roasting pan on top. This goes wonderfully with a vermicelli pilaf (page 108).

SERVES 4

Baked Kofte

Kofte are usually just fried, but here is a baked variation with a spiced tomato sauce.

1 **slice of bread**

⅓ **cup milk**

7 **ounces ground beef**

7 **ounces ground pork**

1 **onion, grated**

1 **garlic clove, minced**

3 **tablespoons finely chopped fresh parsley**

1 **large egg**

½ **teaspoon ground cumin**

¼ **teaspoon hot red chili flakes**

¼ **teaspoon sweet paprika**

sea salt and freshly ground pepper

3–4 **tablespoons all-purpose flour**

4 **tablespoons olive oil**

FOR THE SAUCE

2 **tablespoons olive oil**

3 **large tomatoes, chopped**

2 **tablespoons tomato paste**

1 **teaspoon sweet paprika**

sea salt and freshly ground pepper

2 **tablespoons fresh oregano leaves**

Preheat the oven to 400°F.

To make the kofte

Soak the bread in the milk. Squeeze the excess milk from the bread and crumble into a bowl. Add the ground beef, ground pork, onion, garlic, parsley, egg, cumin, hot red chili flakes and paprika. Combine well and season. Split the mixture into 12 equal amounts, shape into balls, flatten slightly, then dust with the flour.

Heat the olive oil in a nonstick pan over medium-high heat. Cook the meatballs for 3 minutes on each side until lightly browned, then transfer them to a small baking dish.

To make the sauce

Using the same pan that you used to fry the kofte, mix together the olive oil, tomatoes, tomato paste and paprika. Season and cook over low heat for 5 minutes, stirring all the time. Finally, add the oregano and pour over the meatballs in the casserole dish.

Bake for 20 minutes, until the sauce is bubbling. Serve hot.

SERVES 4

Honey and Za'atar Glazed Chicken with Salsify and Cauliflower Puree

The salsify season varies, but it is generally available in the spring. Salsify is a light and milky vegetable that is wonderful used in soups and vegetable purees. The leaves are perfect for salads. The roots themselves, which look like dirty wooden sticks, are not the most attractive but they are delicious. You'll need to peel them to reveal the beige-white skin, immediately placing the vegetable in a bowl of water and lemon juice to prevent them from discoloring before cooking.

Known in Turkey as tekesakall, *salsify is very popular in the country and is sometimes known as the oyster plant due to its delicate flavor and very light oyster taste.*

This recipe is based on a dish I had in Ankara, and when in season, salsify becomes a key ingredient in pilafs, soups and böreks.

FOR THE CHICKEN

- 1 small chicken, about 3 pounds
- sea salt and freshly ground pepper
- ⅓ cup honey
- ¼ cup Za'atar (page 249)
- 3 tablespoons peeled and grated fresh ginger
- 1 teaspoon ground cumin
- 4 tablespoons unsalted butter, melted

FOR THE PUREE

- 11 ounces salsify
- 2 cups coarsely chopped cauliflower
- ¾ cup milk
- sea salt and freshly ground pepper
- 3 tablespoons unsalted butter
- 2 tablespoons heavy cream
- 2 tablespoons finely chopped fresh oregano

To cook the chicken

Preheat the oven to 400°F.

Put the chicken on a rack in a roasting pan and season inside and out. Combine the honey, za'atar, ginger and cumin in a bowl. Brush the mixture all over the chicken, drizzle with melted butter and add a little water to the pan. Roast for about 1½ hours, basting about 1¼ hours, or until an instant-read thermometer inserted in the thigh reads 170°F. Let stand for 20 minutes.

To make the puree

Trim, peel and chop the salsify. Immediately place it in a saucepan with the cauliflower, milk and ¾ cup water and season. Bring to a boil, then reduce to a simmer for 20 minutes, until tender. Drain the salsify and cauliflower, then puree in a food processor with the butter and cream until it is smooth and creamy. Stir in the oregano.

To serve

Carve the chicken and serve with the salsify and cauliflower puree.

SERVES 4

Spice Scented Spring Lamb with Quince and Mustard Relish

- 2 large quinces, peeled, cored and sliced
- 6 tablespoons port
- 2 teaspoons dry mustard
- ½ teaspoon ground cloves
- ¼ teaspoon ground nutmeg

FOR THE LAMB

- ½ teaspoon ground cumin
- ½ teaspoon ground cardamom
- ¼ teaspoon ground coriander
- ¼ teaspoon ground cinnamon
   sea salt and freshly ground pepper
- 1 pound boneless lamb loin, in 1 piece
- 2 tablespoons olive oil
- 2 cups shelled fava beans
- 1 tablespoon unsalted butter
- ¼ cup fresh mint leaves, plus more for garnish

To make the relish

Place the quinces in a saucepan with the port, bring to the boil, then reduce the heat and simmer for 35–40 minutes, until the consistency is like jam. Add the mustard, cloves and nutmeg and mix well. Cover and set aside until ready to serve.

4 hours in advance

Make a spice rub by combining the cumin, cardamom, cilantro, cinnamon, ½ teaspoon salt and ¼ teaspoon pepper in a bowl. Season the lamb with the spice rub and refrigerate for around 4 hours.

To cook the lamb

Sauté the lamb in the oil in a skillet over medium heat for about 15 minutes, turning occasionally, or until an instant-read thermometer inserted in the center reads 125°F. Remove from the heat and let stand 5 minutes.

Meanwhile, bring a small saucepan of water to a boil and cook the fava beans for 3–4 minutes. Drain and cool. Remove the skins if you wish.

In another small pan melt the butter and sauté ¼ cup of the mint leaves until just wilted, then add the fava beans and cook for 3 minutes more. Finally add the meat juices from the skillet, and season.

To serve

Slice the lamb into 16 pieces, and season. Cover with foil to keep warm. Divide the bean mixture evenly, spooning into the centers of 4 dinner plates. Top each with 4 slices of lamb. Garnish with fresh mint leaves and serve with the quince relish.

SERVES 4

Pomegranate Glazed Kebabs with Spiced Pomegranate Chutney

I love the sweet and sour flavors added to tender lamb, as shown in this light and zingy riff on the classic Turkish kebab.

¾ cup pomegranate juice

3 tablespoons Pomegranate Molasses (page 249)

4 garlic cloves, minced

4 juniper berries, crushed

10 pink peppercorns, crushed

1¾ pounds boneless leg of lamb, cut into 1-inch cubes

FOR THE CHUTNEY

seeds from 2 pomegranates

4 scallions, finely sliced

1 orange, peeled and cut into small pieces

2 tablespoons orange juice

3 tablespoons finely chopped fresh mint

1 fresh hot red chili, seeded and minced

¼ teaspoon cayenne pepper

¼ teaspoon sweet paprika

sea salt and freshly ground pepper

FOR THE GLAZE

¼ cup Pomegranate Molasses (page 249)

juice of 1 lemon

1 tablespoon honey

1 garlic clove, minced

12 wooden skewers, soaked

1 day in advance

In a large bowl combine the pomegranate juice and molasses, garlic, juniper berries and pink peppercorns. Add the lamb and mix well. Refrigerate for at least 2 hours or ideally overnight.

2 hours in advance

Combine the pomegranate seeds, scallions, orange and orange juice, mint, chili, cayenne and sweet paprika in a bowl, season and refrigerate for a couple of hours.

To make the glaze

Combine all the ingredients and keep until you are ready to cook the lamb.

To cook the lamb

Preheat the broiler. Remove the lamb cubes from the marinade, thread evenly onto the skewers, and brush with the glaze. Broil, turning frequently and basting with the glaze every now and again, about 10 minutes for medium-rare. Serve immediately with the pomegranate chutney.

SERVES 6

Veal Ragù in Eggplants

2 tablespoons olive oil

1¾ pounds boneless veal shoulder, cut into ¾-inch pieces

2 onions, finely chopped

2 garlic cloves, minced

sea salt and freshly ground pepper

3 ripe tomatoes, cubed

1 long red sweet pepper such as Cubanelle, seeded and chopped

½ teaspoon sweet paprika

½ teaspoon crushed Aleppo pepper

1¾ cups veal stock

6 small eggplants, about 10 ounces each

½ cup vegetable oil, as needed

6 (1½– to 2-cup) ramekins

Preheat the oven to 400°F.

To make the ragù

Heat the olive oil in a nonstick pan over medium-high heat. Sauté the veal, onions and garlic for 10 minutes. Season, then stir in the tomatoes, pepper, paprika and Aleppo pepper. Pour in the veal stock and cook over medium-low heat for about 1½ hours, until the veal is tender and the mixture has formed a thick sauce.

To prepare the eggplants

Cut each eggplant lengthwise into 6 slices. Heat the vegetable oil in a nonstick pan over medium-high heat and fry the eggplant, a few slices at a time, adding more oil for each batch, about 2 minutes per side, until golden brown. Transfer to paper towels to drain.

Line each ramekin with 6 eggplant slices, each slice slightly overlapping the preceding one, and overhanging the edge of the ramekin. Spoon the veal ragù into each ramekin and fold over the ends of the eggplant to form a lid. Reserve the leftover ragù for serving.

Bake the ramekins for 10 minutes, until the eggplant is tender.

To serve

Carefully turn each ramekin upside down onto the middle of individual dinner plates, and spoon the remaining ragù over each serving.

SERVES 6

Poussin with Yogurt and Tarragon Sauce

Many dishes in Eastern Mediterranean cuisine are cooked with stabilized yogurt, producing wonderfully light dishes that are very healthy. This was something that I had never done before, but at the Al Halabi, Four Seasons, restaurant in Damascus, cooking with stabilized yogurt is one of their specialties. So I'm very pleased to be able to adopt this method, one of the oldest in Eastern Mediterranean cooking, for this very contemporary dish.

The yogurt is stabilized by heating with egg and cornstarch. But take extra care not to let the mixture come to a boil.

FOR THE POUSSINS

- 4 **poussins, about 14 ounces each**
- **sea salt and freshly ground black pepper**
- 2 **tablespoons clarified butter or ghee**
- 2 **tablespoons finely chopped tarragon**

FOR THE SAUCE

- 1¾ **cups high-quality yogurt**
- 1¼ **cups chicken stock**
- 1 **small egg, beaten**
- 3 **garlic cloves, minced**
- 2 **pinches sea salt**
- ½ **teaspoon freshly ground white pepper**
- 1 **tablespoon cornstarch**
- 4 **tablespoons finely chopped fresh tarragon**
- ⅓ **cup olive oil**

To cook the poussins

Preheat the oven to 400°F. Place the poussins in a roasting pan, then season and drizzle with the butter. Sprinkle the tarragon over the birds and add ½ cup water to the pan. Roast for 45 minutes to an hour, basting every now and again, until golden brown and an instant-read thermometer inserted in the breast reads 165°F.

To make the sauce

Combine the yogurt, stock, egg, garlic, salt and white pepper in a saucepan; do not heat yet. Whisk the cornstarch and add ¼ cup water in a small bowl to make a smooth paste, then add to the saucepan. Now cook over medium-low heat for 12–15 minutes, stirring all the time, until lightly thickened, but not boiling. Remove from the heat and add the roasting juices from the poussins.

Puree half the tarragon in a food processor. Transfer to a small bowl and stir in the remaining tarragon and the olive oil. Add to the yogurt sauce.

To serve

Cut each poussin in half, arrange on a serving plate and spoon over some yogurt and tarragon sauce. Serve with rice.

SERVES 4

Al Halabi Style Kebabs
with Walnuts and Pine Nuts
Served with Potato Moutabel

*Mohamed Hussein of the Al Halabi, Four Seasons, in Damascus is considered
to be one of the best chefs in Syria, and that in a country where just about
everyone considers themselves to be a good chef! These kebabs, made from a
recipe he gave me, are best grilled outdoors, but they are also lovely cooked in a
stovetop grill pan or simply broiled.*

FOR THE KEBABS

- 18 ounces finely ground lamb
- 1 small red bell pepper, seeded and finely chopped
- 1 cup finely chopped mushrooms
- 1 cup (4 ounces) finely chopped mozzarella
- ½ cup coarsely chopped pine nuts
- ½ cup coarsely chopped walnuts
- 1 teaspoon dried mint
- ½ teaspoon sea salt
- ½ teaspoon ground white pepper

FOR THE MOUTABEL

- 2 large baking potatoes, scrubbed but unpeeled
- 3 tablespoons lemon juice
- 2 tablespoons tahini
- 2 tablespoons yogurt
- ½ teaspoon ground cumin
  sea salt and freshly ground pepper
- ½ tablespoon hemp seeds

- 8 long skewers, ideally flat metal skewers

To make the kebabs

Combine all the ingredients in a bowl. Knead in the bowl for
10 minutes until it resembles a sticky dough.

Shape the kebabs onto flat metal skewers, using about
3 tablespoons for each, shaping the meat around the top end of
the skewer. Freeze for 20 minutes.

Build a hot fire in an outdoor grill. Remove the kebabs from the
freezer. Grill for 6–8 minutes, turning occasionally, until browned.

To make the moutabel

Cook the potatoes in a large saucepan of lightly salted water over
medium heat until tender, about 30 minutes. Drain and transfer
to a bowl. Coarsely mash the potatoes with their skins. Add the
lemon juice, tahini, yogurt and cumin. Season and sprinkle with
the hemp seeds.

Slide the meat off the skewers and serve with the potato moutabel.

SERVES 4

Aleppo Pepper Marinated Chicken Kebab

Aleppo peppers give this marinade a mild kick. The ice cubes are used to create the proper thickness of the marinade.

⅓ cup tomato paste

3 tablespoons lemon juice

1 teaspoon crushed Aleppo pepper

3 garlic cloves, minced

½ teaspoon freshly ground white pepper

½ teaspoon sea salt

3 ice cubes

¼ cup vegetable oil

4 boneless and skinless chicken breasts, cut into 1-inch cubes

8 skewers

1 day in advance

In a food processor fitted with the metal chopping blade, combine the tomato paste, lemon juice, Aleppo pepper, garlic, white pepper, salt and ice cubes. Drizzle in the oil a little at a time as you process, until you get a thick paste. Place the chicken in a bowl and coat well with the paste. Cover and refrigerate overnight.

On the day

To cook, build a hot fire in an outdoor grill. Scrape the marinade off the chicken (discarding the paste) and arrange the chicken cubes on skewers. Grill for 8–10 minutes, turning to cook evenly on all sides. (The chicken skewers can also be broiled.)

Serve with Baba Ghanoush (page 53).

SERVES 4

Jidi Bel Zet – Veal Shank with Saffron and Seven Spice

This dish is normally made with kid – baby goat – and comes from an ancient Damascene recipe. I tried it in a restaurant in the old city. It wasn't actually on the menu, but I went there so many times on various trips that the chef/owner asked me why I was in Syria so much. When I told him I was there to learn more authentic Syrian cooking, he insisted that I return the next day so he could prepare jidi bel zet in my honor. I couldn't turn down such an invitation, and it was a worthwhile discovery. Here's my interpretation of what he taught me.

4 **veal shanks, cut about 1½ inches thick**

2 **tablespoons all-purpose flour**

8 **tablespoons olive oil**

1 **tablespoon Baharat (page 248)**

3 **bay leaves**

3 **medium sweet potatoes, peeled and cubed**

2 **shallots, finely chopped**

2 **garlic cloves, minced**

sea salt and freshly ground pepper

pinch of **saffron**

juice of ½ **lemon**

Preheat the oven to 350°F.

Dust the veal shanks with the flour. Heat 3 tablespoons of the olive oil in a large casserole dish. Add the veal shanks, sprinkle with the baharat and add the bay leaves. Sauté for 5–8 minutes, turning the shanks to cook evenly, until golden brown on all sides. Add 3½ cups water, cover and bake for 1 hour 30 minutes, until the meat is tender and coming away from the bone. Once cooked, remove the veal shanks from the dish with a slotted spoon. Put the cooking liquid aside for the sauce.

Meanwhile, heat 3 tablespoons olive oil in a nonstick skillet and sauté the sweet potatoes for 5–6 minutes, until golden in color. Remove from the skillet and set aside.

Heat the remaining 2 tablespoons olive oil in a large nonstick saucepan over medium heat. Sauté the shallots and garlic for 1–2 minutes, until softened. Season and add the saffron and browned sweet potato. Pour in the cooking liquid and add the veal shanks. Cook for 10 minutes, until the potatoes are tender. Just before serving, add the lemon juice. Serve with saffron rice.

SERVES 4

Yiahni – Slow-Cooked Lamb with Scallions, Dried Cherries and Lemon

Yiahni, a light Turkish stew, is something very special that my mother makes for me as a special treat when the first of the spring scallions are out and the new-season lamb has arrived. It's cooked slowly with plenty of seasonal greens – you can add spinach if you like. The addition of cherries is my touch, giving the dish a sweet and sour flavor. Slow it may be, but this dish is well worth waiting for!

3 **tablespoons olive oil**

1¾ **pounds boneless lamb shoulder, cut into 1-inch cubes**

24 **scallions, finely sliced**

1⅓ **cups lamb stock**

grated zest and juice of 2 **lemons**

3 **tablespoons dried cherries**

3 **tablespoons coarsely chopped fresh parsley**

2 **tablespoons pine nuts, toasted**

Heat the olive oil in a large nonstick sauté pan. Brown the lamb for 3–5 minutes, turning to ensure even cooking. Then add the scallions and cook for 5 minutes more. Add the stock, and lemon zest and juice. Cover and simmer over low heat for 1½ hours, until the meat is tender. Add the dried cherries and stir in the parsley.

Serve in deep plates, topped with pine nuts and accompanied by a simple pilaf.

SERVES 4

Abu Basti – Lamb, Winter Squash and Tahini

Another ancient dish I discovered in Damascus, which isn't even known to the native Damascenes, was shown to me by Chef Mazin at Safran restaurant. It's a dish that he says has been passed down many maternal generations of his family. Every Syrian family has their own version – here's mine. Use any kind of firm winter squash — butternut, Hubbard and kabocha are options.

1 **pound boneless leg of lamb, cut into 1-inch cubes**

2 **tablespoons clarified butter or ghee**

1 **onion, finely chopped**

2 **garlic cloves, minced**

2 **bay leaves**

2 **pounds winter squash, peeled, seeded and cut into 1-inch cubes**

3 **tablespoons olive oil**

sea salt and freshly ground pepper

3 **cups yogurt**

1 **egg yolk**

2–3 **tablespoons tahini**

¾ **cup baldo or Arborio rice**

Preheat the oven to 400°F.

In a large saucepan, sauté the lamb in the butter over medium heat for 3–4 minutes, until just golden brown. Add the onion, garlic, bay leaves and 3¼ cups water. Cover and reduce the heat to low. Simmer for about 1 hour, until the meat is tender. Remove the meat with a slotted spoon and reserve the cooking liquid.

Arrange the squash on a baking sheet, drizzle with the olive oil and season. Roast about 20 minutes until the squash is tender and golden around the edges.

In a separate large nonstick saucepan, whisk the yogurt and egg yolk and season. Add 1 cup of the cooking liquid and cook for 10–12 minutes over low heat, stirring constantly without boiling, until lightly thickened. Add the squash, lamb and tahini.

Meanwhile bring 1½ cups of the cooking liquid and the rice to a boil in a small saucepan. Cover and simmer over low heat until tender, about 17 minutes. If you need to, add more water while cooking.

Serve the stew with the rice.

SERVES 4

Potato and Green Chili Stuffed Kofte in Tomato Sauce

FOR THE STUFFING

- 2 **tablespoons olive oil**
- 2 **baking potatoes, peeled and finely diced**
- 2 **fresh green chilies, seeded and finely chopped**
- 1 **onion, grated**
- 3 **tablespoons finely chopped fresh cilantro**
- 2 **garlic cloves, minced**
- 1¾ **cups (4 ounces) shredded haloumi or mozzarella cheese**

FOR THE KOFTE

- **sea salt and freshly ground pepper**
- 18 **ounces ground lamb**
- 3 **tablespoons olive oil**

FOR THE SAUCE

- 1 **tablespoon olive oil**
- 1 **garlic clove, minced**
- 4 **large ripe tomatoes, skinned and pureed**
- 1 **tablespoon tomato paste**
- ½ **teaspoon ground cumin**
- **sea salt and freshly ground pepper**

TO SERVE

- 3 **tablespoons finely chopped fresh cilantro**
- ½ **cup pine nuts, toasted and coarsely chopped**

Preheat the oven to 400°F.

To make the stuffing

Heat the olive oil in a pan over medium heat. Sauté the potatoes, chilies, onion, cilantro and garlic for 8–10 minutes, until the potato is cooked. Remove from the heat and let cool. Stir in the haloumi.

To make the kofte

Season the lamb and place in a food processor. Pulse a few times to get a smooth texture. For each kofte, flatten a walnut-sized portion of the lamb mixture. Add a spoonful of stuffing. Fold the meat over the stuffing and roll to enclose. Repeat with the remaining meat and stuffing.

Heat the oil in a nonstick ovenproof pan over medium-high heat and brown the kofte on all sides, about 4 minutes.

To make the sauce

Heat the oil in a nonstick skillet. Sauté the garlic for 1 minute, then add the tomatoes, tomato paste and cumin. Cook for 5 minutes more. Pour the sauce over the kofte, season and bake for 12–15 minutes.

Serve hot, sprinkled with the cilantro and pine nuts.

SERVES 4

Za'atar and Pistachio Crusted Poussin with Quince and Rose Jam

FOR THE JAM

- 2 quinces, peeled and shredded
- grated zest and juice of ½ small lemon
- 2 cups sugar
- 3 tablespoons dried rose petals

FOR THE POUSSINS

- 4 poussins, about 14 ounces each
- 3 tablespoons unsalted butter, softened
- sea salt and freshly ground pepper
- 4 tablespoons Za'atar (page 249)
- 1 cup ground pistachios

At least 1 day in advance

Place 2 cups water in a large saucepan and bring to a boil. Add the quinces, lemon zest and juice. Simmer for 15 minutes, then add the sugar and bring back to a boil for 1 minute. Reduce the heat to medium and add the rose petals. Simmer for 1 hour, until the quince has turned a pink color and thickened to a jam consistency. Pour into a hot sterilized jar and refrigerate until ready to use.

On the day

Preheat the oven to 400°F.

Halve the poussins and rub generously with the butter, then season. Combine the za'atar and pistachios in a bowl, and rub over the poussins. Place in a roasting pan, adding ½ cup water, and roast for about 50 minutes, basting from time to time, until golden brown and an instant-read thermometer inserted in the breast reads 165°F. Let stand at room temperature for 5 minutes.

Serve the poussins hot, with a spoonful of the quince and rose jam.

SERVES 4

Orange and Mustard Marinated Chicken

A fragrant, citrusy, summery dish, delicious served with a mustard green leaf salad and buttered baby potatoes.

FOR THE MARINADE

grated zest
of 2 **oranges**

²⁄₃ **cup orange juice**

1 **tablespoon Dijon mustard**

1 **tablespoon white wine vinegar**

1 **tablespoon light brown sugar**

FOR THE CHICKEN

4 **chicken breast halves, with skin and bones**

2 **tablespoons olive oil**

sea salt and freshly ground pepper

FOR THE SALAD

1 **tablespoon white wine vinegar**

sea salt and freshly ground pepper

2 **blood oranges, segmented**

1 **avocado, pitted, peeled and sliced**

7 **ounces mustard greens**

7 **ounces green beans, blanched**

1 day in advance

Combine all the marinade ingredients in a bowl and whisk well. Place the chicken breasts in a nonreactive dish and pour over half the marinade. Cover and refrigerate overnight, and store the remaining marinade in a separate container.

On the day

Preheat the oven to 400°F.

Bring the chicken to room temperature. Drain off and discard the marinade. Brush the chicken with oil and cook over high heat in a large skillet for about 3 minutes on each side, until evenly browned. Transfer the chicken to an ovenproof dish and season. Bake about 30 minutes, until an instant-read thermometer inserted in the thickest part of a breast reads 165°F.

To make the salad

To make the dressing, whisk the vinegar into the reserved marinade and season. Place the oranges, avocado, mustard greens and beans in a bowl and toss with the dressing.

Serve the chicken with the salad, accompanied by hot baby potatoes tossed in butter.

SERVES 4

Kadaifi Schnitzel with Pomegranate Sauce

My new family favorite! I had this on my last trip to Istanbul, at a very modern café. I loved this great idea, as back home I make schnitzel at least once a week. I would love to have been the one to think of it! I prefer to use chicken, but veal or pork works well too. Kadaifi pastry is like a shredded filo pastry, and by pomegranate sauce I mean a simple pomegranate molasses, just a drizzle, nothing more than that.

7 ounces kadaifi pastry, thawed

¼ cup all-purpose flour, for dusting

2 large eggs

4 skinless and boneless chicken breast halves

3 tablespoons olive oil

2 tablespoons clarified butter or ghee

6 tablespoons Pomegranate Molasses (page 249)

Allow the kadaifi to dry a little at room temperature for 5–6 minutes, then place in a dish or on a plate and crush slightly using your hands, to get small broken pieces. Place the flour in a separate dish and beat the eggs in a third dish.

Using a heavy kitchen mallet, beat the chicken breasts as thinly as you can. Dip each chicken fillet into the flour, then into the eggs, and finally roll it in the kadaifi pieces. Heat the oil and butter together in a large skillet over medium heat. Sauté the chicken for 3–4 minutes on each side, until crisp golden brown. Transfer to paper towels to drain briefly.

Place on dinner plates, drizzle with the pomegranate molasses and serve with White Butter Bean, Feta and Za'atar Spread (page 33).

SERVES 4

Lavender and Honey Glazed Chicken with Pine Nut, Chervil and Honey Sauce

Chervil is the most elegant of herbs. It combines a light anise fragrance with parsley's cleansing freshness. The leaves are delicate and are perfect in sauces or soups. If unavailable, use parsley.

FOR THE CHICKEN

- 3 tablespoons Madeira
- 1 teaspoon dried lavender flowers
- 5 tablespoons honey
  sea salt and freshly ground pepper
- 4 chicken breast halves, with skin and bones

FOR THE SAUCE

- ¾ cup pine nuts, lightly toasted
- 3 tablespoons finely chopped fresh chervil
- 2 tablespoons olive oil
- 2 tablespoons honey
  sea salt and freshly ground pepper

An hour in advance

Pour the Madeira into a saucepan, add the lavender flowers and honey, bring to a boil, then reduce to a simmer for 2 minutes. Let stand for an hour so that the flavors infuse, then season.

To cook the chicken

Preheat the oven to 400°F.

Arrange the chicken breasts in a broiler pan and brush with some of the honey and lavender mixture. Roast for 45 to 50 minutes, until golden brown and an instant-read thermometer inserted in the thickest part reads 165°F. Reserve some of the cooking juices for the sauce.

To make the sauce

In a large bowl combine the pine nuts, chervil, olive oil, honey and 3 tablespoons of the cooking juices from the chicken, then season.

Serve the chicken with the sauce.

SERVES 4

FISH

Ma'alula is an awe-inspiring place, its ancient past seeming to reflect from its whitewashed walls, hidden within the nooks and crannies of intricate alleyways along which its inhabitants have wandered for more than two millennia, and to echo within the caves and grottos.

In a predominantly Muslim country, the village is home to two ancient Christian monasteries: St. Sergius and St. Thecla. Thecla was a disciple of St. Paul and it is believed that she is buried in the mountain just above the monastery.

While I was visiting the monastery of St. Thecla, I was very honored to be invited to share lunch with Mother Belagia and the rest of the nuns. The monastery, dedicated to caring for orphans, prepares a large quantity of food every day in its vast kitchens, which are filled with warmth and the luscious smells of herbs and spices. I personally cannot lay claim to having any particular faith, though I do believe in God, but to see these nuns at work, kneading the breads, preparing the rice dishes for the poor and the needy, filled my heart, for their humility is humbling.

Vine Leaves Stuffed with Smoked Haddock and Tarragon

It was in the monastery of St. Thecla that I met Sister Agia from Laconia. She had prepared this dish, which originates from her native Greece. The traditional recipe is usually made with salt cod, a staple of that region, but I've used smoked haddock with the rice, to create a sort of kedgeree wrapped in vine leaves.

FOR THE VINE LEAVES

50 **fresh or preserved vine leaves**

To prepare the vine leaves

If you are fortunate enough to be able to find fresh vine leaves, then use them. Select the 40 best leaves, and set the remaining 10 leaves aside. Bring a saucepan of water to a boil. Add the leaves and cook 30 seconds for preserved leaves and 5 minutes for fresh. Drain and pat dry with paper towels.

1¼ **pounds smoked haddock (see note)**

4 **tablespoons olive oil**

12 **scallions, finely sliced**

1 **large tomato, finely chopped**

1 **tablespoon finely chopped fresh tarragon**

¼ **cup long-grain rice**

sea salt and freshly ground pepper

To make the haddock filling

Flake the haddock, removing the skin and ensuring there are no remaining bones. Put half the oil into a saucepan over medium heat and sauté the scallions with the tomato and tarragon for 2 minutes. Add the flaked haddock and stir to combine, then add the rice. Season and add ½ cup of water. Cover and simmer for 5 minutes, until the rice is barely tender. Let cool.

To cook the vine leaves

To prepare the stuffed leaves, lay out a cooled, blanched leaf, shiny side down, and place a small amount of the smoked haddock mixture in the center – just enough to still be able to comfortably wrap the leaf around the mixture. Fold the bottom edge nearest you over the filling, then fold in the two sides and tightly roll away from you into a neat parcel.

Line the bottom of a medium-sized saucepan with 4 or 5 of the unblanched leaves that you put aside. Arrange the stuffed vine leaves, seam side down, in the prepared saucepan, keeping them nice and tight in layers. Pour on the remaining 2 tablespoons olive oil and ¾ cup of water. Arrange the remaining unblanched leaves on top of the stuffed parcels. Weigh the parcels down with a plate to keep them in place, and gently simmer over low heat for 30 minutes.

The vine leaves will keep a better shape if you let them cool slightly before serving.

MAKES 40, SERVES 6–8

Note: Smoked haddock is available at well-stocked fishmongers and online.

Sardines Stuffed with Garlic Scapes, Tomatoes and Za'atar

In Britain, I make this with wild garlic, which, surprisingly, is different from the American variety. Garlic scapes (actually fresh, young garlic stems) are a good substitute, and available at many farmers' markets during their late spring season.

1¾ **pounds whole fresh sardines**

juice of 1 **lemon**

sea salt and freshly ground pepper

4 **tablespoons olive oil**

½ **cup finely chopped garlic scapes**

1 **teaspoon Za'atar (page 249)**

3 **large ripe tomatoes, finely chopped**

3 **tablespoons chopped fresh basil**

3 **tablespoons fresh coarse bread crumbs**

Preheat the oven to 400°F.

Clean the sardines, removing the heads, the guts and the bones, or ask your fish purveyor to do it. Rub lemon juice all over the fish, inside and out, and season.

Put a tablespoon of the olive oil into a pan and sauté the garlic scapes over medium heat, stirring until tender, about 3 minutes. Pour into a bowl. Add the za'atar, tomatoes, basil and bread crumbs, and combine well. Spoon some of the filling into each sardine. Secure with wooden toothpicks and arrange on a baking sheet.

Drizzle with the remaining oil. Bake for 12–15 minutes, or until the sardine flesh is opaque.

SERVES 4

Porgy with Currants and Pistachios and a Blood Orange Sauce

This recipe is close to my heart. When I was growing up we had a walnut tree in the garden of our house in the mountains and it was from that tree that my mother and grandmother would prepare a dish very similar to this one with fresh or preserved nuts. These days, I prefer the green color and buttery flavor of pistachios.

FOR THE PORGY

- 4 **whole porgy (about 1¼ pounds each), cleaned**
- **sea salt and freshly ground pepper**
- 1½ **cups coarsely chopped pistachios**
- 6 **ripe plum tomatoes, finely chopped**
- 1 **small red onion, finely chopped**
- 3 **garlic cloves, minced**
- 4 **tablespoons dried currants**
- 1 **tablespoon Za'atar (page 249)**
- 4 **tablespoons olive oil**

FOR THE SAUCE

- grated zest and juice of 2 **blood oranges**
- ⅓ **cup olive oil**
- **sea salt and freshly ground pepper**

To cook the porgy

Preheat the oven to 400°F.

Season the fish, inside and out.

Combine the pistachios, 4 of the tomatoes, the onion, garlic, currants and za'atar in a bowl. Fill each fish with the mixture and secure with a wooden toothpick. Place the fish on a baking sheet, drizzle with the oil and sprinkle with the remaining 2 tomatoes. Bake for 30–40 minutes, until the fish flesh is opaque when flaked with the tip of a knife.

To make the sauce

In a bowl, combine the orange zest and juice with the oil, and season. Pour a little over the fish just before serving.

SERVES 4

Sea Bass with Garlic Scapes
en Papillote Poached in Raki

Raki, with slight variations of spelling, is a common anise apéritif enjoyed across much of the Eastern Mediterranean. It was my father's favorite, and I always found it fascinating to watch it turn from a greenish color to milky white when water was added.

Mezze and raki go hand in hand, though here it is employed as part of a main-course recipe. You can use white wine if you can't get hold of raki or are not too keen on the anise flavor.

4 sea bass fillets (6 ounces each)

4 tablespoons lemon juice

4 tablespoons olive oil

½ cup finely chopped garlic scapes (see page 169)

2 ripe plum tomatoes, sliced into 12 rounds

12 pearl onions, peeled

4 lemon slices

4 bay leaves

2 teaspoons crushed sumac

4 tablespoons raki, pastis, or ouzo

sea salt and freshly ground pepper

Preheat the oven to 400°F.

Have ready four 16-inch square pieces of parchment paper. For each serving, place a fillet in the center of the bottom half of a parchment square. Drizzle with 1 tablespoon each of the lemon juice and the olive oil and 2 tablespoons of the garlic scapes. Add 3 tomato rounds, 3 pearl onions, 1 slice of lemon and 1 bay leaf. Sprinkle with ½ teaspoon of sumac, then 1 tablespoon of raki; season. Fold the paper in half, then tightly crimp the three open sides to create a parcel. Transfer the parcels to baking sheets.

Bake until the parcels look slightly puffed and the fish is opaque (open a parcel to check), about 25 minutes. Place each parcel on a dinner plate and serve immediately, allowing each guest to open his or her own parcel.

SERVES 4

Zucchini Flowers Stuffed with Crab and Shrimp

The flowers of the zucchini plant are delicate and pale, but unfortunately their season is short – July to August – and you might have to search for them at your farmers' market. The smaller flowers can be cooked tempura-style, but the larger ones, common in Italian cuisine, can be stuffed with cheese and deep-fried. When preparing zucchini flowers before stuffing, carefully cut out and discard the stigma and stamens, as they can be bitter. Serve with a simple green salad.

FOR THE ZUCCHINI

- 12 **zucchini flowers**
- 8 **ounces crab meat**
- 4 **ounces cooked shrimp, finely chopped**
- 1 **cup ricotta**
- 3 **tablespoons grated Pecorino Romano**
- 2 **tablespoons finely chopped oregano**
- **vegetable oil, for frying**
- **all-purpose flour, for dusting**

FOR THE BATTER

- ⅔ **cup all-purpose flour**
- ½ **teaspoon sea salt**
- 3 **ice cubes**

To prepare the zucchini flowers

Carefully open the flowers and remove the stigma and stamens.

Combine the crab, shrimp, ricotta and Pecorino Romano in a bowl, then fold in the oregano. Spoon a small amount of the mixture into each flower and gently twist the petals to seal in the stuffing.

To make the batter

Using a fork, barely combine the flour, salt, ⅓ cup water and ice cubes – a smooth batter is not required.

To cook the zucchini flowers

Pour enough oil into a large saucepan to come halfway up the sides, and heat over high heat to 375°F. Preheat the oven to 200°F.

In three batches, dust each stuffed flower with flour, dip them into the batter, then gently drop them into the hot oil. Cook about 2½ minutes, until golden brown. Using a slotted spoon, transfer to paper towels to drain. Keep warm in the oven.

Serve hot.

SERVES 6

Warm Shrimp Salad with Pink Radish and Red Onion

If you wish to make this a really special summer salad, top with nasturtium flowers and sumac.

FOR THE SALAD

- 8 small pink radishes, finely sliced
- 7 ounces arugula
- 1 red onion, sliced
- ¼ cup fennel fronds
- 2 tablespoons olive oil
- 12 jumbo shrimp, peeled, tail section intact

  sea salt and freshly ground pepper
- ¼ cup pine nuts, lightly toasted

FOR THE DRESSING

- 2 tablespoons olive oil
- 2 tablespoons orange juice
- 2 tablespoons red wine vinegar
- 1 teaspoon Za'atar (page 249)
- 2 teaspoons finely chopped fresh cilantro

  sea salt and freshly ground pepper

To make the salad

Combine the radishes, arugula, onion and fennel fronds in a large bowl. Heat the oil in a heavy pan over medium heat. Add the shrimp and cook for 2 minutes on each side, until the shrimp are opaque. Season and keep warm.

To make the dressing

Combine all the ingredients, and season.

To serve

Serve the salad on 4 plates and sprinkle with the pine nuts. Top each portion with 3 shrimp and drizzle with the dressing.

SERVES 4

Sautéed Monkfish with Rose Petal Salt

This recipe works beautifully with scallops too. It was chef Martin from the Al Halabi, Four Seasons, in Damascus who told me about fish with rose petal salt. I tried it and loved it, so now I keep rose petal salt in my cupboard next to my regular salt. Serve with the Pilaf with Vermicelli and the Tomato, Pomegranate and Sumac Salad (pages 108 and 126).

petals of 1 **large unsprayed red rose, washed and dried**

2 **tablespoons flaky sea salt, such as Maldon or** *fleur de sel*

1½ **pounds monkfish fillet**

2 **tablespoons olive oil**

1 **tablespoon clarified butter or ghee**

At least 1 day in advance

Place the petals and salt on a platter and rub together until the petals are well mashed. The petals will break up and color the salt. I like a chunky texture so I don't overwork the mixture; and whatever you do, don't be tempted to place it in a blender, as you will end up with a puree. Transfer to a jar and let stand at least overnight to infuse the flavors.

On the day

Cut the monkfish into 12 chunky pieces. Lightly oil the fish. Heat the clarified butter in a large skillet. Add the fish and cook, turning once, about 2½ minutes, or until golden brown. Serve topped with a generous pinch of the rose petal salt sprinkled on top. Serve hot.

SERVES 4

Vine-Wrapped Steamed Turbot with Yogurt, Walnut and Dill Sauce

Fish with a yogurt-based sauce might seem an unusual combination, but it is commonplace in the coastal regions of Turkey. This also works well with monkfish.

FOR THE TURBOT

- 12 large vine leaves, fresh or preserved
- 4 skinless turbot fillets (7 ounces each), checked for bones
- sea salt and freshly ground pepper
- 4 sprigs fresh dill
- grated zest of 1 lemon

FOR THE SAUCE

- ¾ cup yogurt
- ¾ cup ground walnuts
- 2 teaspoons finely chopped fresh dill
- 1 garlic clove, minced
- sea salt and freshly ground pepper

To cook the turbot

Bring a saucepan of water to a boil. Add the leaves and cook 30 seconds for preserved leaves and 5 minutes for fresh. Drain and pat dry with paper towels.

Prepare a steamer saucepan, partially filled with water, and bring to a simmer over medium heat.

Place a vine leaf, shiny side down, on a work surface in front of you. Slightly overlap another leaf, shiny side down. Finally, place a third leaf in the center.

Place a turbot fillet in the middle of the leaves, then season and top with a dill sprig and a touch of lemon zest. Wrap the fish fillet in the leaves. It's a bit fiddly but ideally you need to completely enclose the fillet by rolling the leaves around it and tucking the edges in. Repeat with the rest of the leaves and fish. Arrange the 4 parcels in the steamer. Cover and steam for 10 minutes, or until the fish under the leaves feels firm when pressed.

To make the sauce

Combine the yogurt, ground walnuts, chopped dill and garlic together in a bowl and season.

Serve the vine-wrapped fish hot with the sauce.

SERVES 4

Shrimp with Orange-Saffron Butter and Rutabaga Tahini Mash

Sweet and delicate shrimp with a lightly perfumed saffron butter – easy, delicious and very quick! A green salad is a nice accompaniment.

FOR THE BUTTER

3	tablespoons dry vermouth
pinch of	saffron
grated zest and juice of ½	orange
grated zest of ½	lemon
8	tablespoons unsalted butter, softened
4	garlic cloves, minced
2	tablespoons finely chopped fresh chives
1	teaspoon ground cumin
½	teaspoon crushed sumac
	sea salt and freshly ground pepper

FOR THE MASH

11	ounces rutabaga (yellow turnip), peeled and chopped
3	tablespoons ground cumin
2	tablespoons tahini
3	garlic cloves, minced
2	tablespoons lemon juice
¼	cup olive oil, as needed
	sea salt and freshly ground pepper

FOR THE SHRIMP

1	tablespoon olive oil
20	jumbo shrimp, shelled and deveined

At least 2 hours in advance

Pour the vermouth into a small bowl and add the saffron. Let stand for 3 minutes, then stir in the orange zest and juice and lemon zest. Add the butter, garlic, chives, cumin and sumac, and season and combine well. Lay out a piece of plastic wrap and shape the butter on the wrap into an 8-inch log. Roll the plastic wrap around the butter and seal well. Refrigerate for a couple of hours, until firm. If you're in a hurry you can put it in the freezer.

To make the mash

Place the rutabaga in a saucepan half filled with water and bring to a boil. Reduce to a simmer and cook for 15–20 minutes, until tender. Drain and process in a food processor until smooth. Transfer to a mixing bowl and combine with the cumin, tahini, garlic, lemon juice and enough olive oil to make a smooth puree; season.

To cook the shrimp

Heat the olive oil in a heavy skillet over medium-high heat. Add the shrimp and cook for 2–3 minutes, stirring all the time, until the shrimp are opaque. Set aside. Add about 6 tablespoons of the orange-saffron butter to the pan, turn off the heat and let it melt.

To serve

For each serving, place 4 shrimp on a warm dinner plate, drizzle with the melted butter and top with a thin slice of the remaining butter. Serve with the rutabaga puree.

SERVES 4

Red Mullet with Pine Nuts, Currants and Gremolata

Gremolata is a garnish or condiment made from parsley, lemon and garlic. It is added to fish or meat dishes to give a more intense flavor. This dish can be prepared using almost any fish, but it turns out particularly well using rich, meaty fish such as mullet.

FOR THE GREMOLATA BREAD CRUMBS

- 1½ **cups fresh bread crumbs**
- 3 **tablespoons finely chopped fresh parsley**
- grated zest of 1 **lemon**
- 2 **garlic cloves, minced**
- ½ **teaspoon freshly ground black pepper**

FOR THE MULLET

- 4 **whole red mullets**
- 3 **tablespoons dried currants**
- 2 **tablespoons pine nuts, toasted and finely chopped**
- grated zest of 1 **lemon**
- juice of ½ **lemon**
- **all-purpose flour, for dusting**
- 2 **large eggs, beaten**
- ¼ **cup olive oil**

To make the gremolata bread crumbs

Combine the bread crumbs, parsley, lemon zest, garlic and pepper in a bowl and set aside.

To cook the mullet

Have the fish purveyor clean and bone the mullets. Combine the currants, pine nuts, lemon zest and juice, and add 3 tablespoons of the gremolata bread crumbs. Place a spoonful of the stuffing inside each fish. Put the flour, eggs and remaining bread crumb mixture into 3 separate shallow dishes. Coat each fish with flour, then dip them in the egg, and finally coat with the bread crumbs.

Heat the olive oil in a large skillet over medium heat. Add the mullets and cook for 8 minutes, turning once, until golden brown, taking care not to let the stuffing fall out. Serve hot.

SERVES 4

Basil and Kadaifi-Wrapped Shrimp with Pine Nut Tarator

Kadaifi is basically shredded filo pastry. It is one of the most popular doughs eaten in Turkey, Syria and Jordan, and is more commonly used in sweet preparations.

This is a personal favorite of mine. It's a showstopper dish – impressive and contemporary, yet so simple to make. You can use the same recipe for wrapping a variety of vegetables too; peppers, eggplant and asparagus are particularly well suited to this. Kadaifi pastry dries very fast, so work quickly and cover it with a damp cloth when you're not using it.

There are many varieties of basil – purple, black, opal, Thai. The best way to store any of these varieties is to keep a bunch in a small glass of water at room temperature, making sure the leaves are kept dry at all times.

FOR THE SHRIMP

- 2 **tablespoons lemon juice**
- 1 **garlic clove, minced**
- ½ **teaspoon ground coriander**
- ½ **tablespoon hot pepper sauce**
- 12 **jumbo shrimp, peeled and deveined**
- **vegetable oil, for deep-frying**

FOR THE TARATOR

- 1 **slice of bread, crusts removed**
- 1½ **cups pine nuts**
- 2 **tablespoons coarsely chopped fresh parsley**
- juice of 1 **lemon**
- 2 **small garlic cloves, minced**
- ¼ **cup olive oil**
- **sea salt and freshly ground pepper**
- 8 **ounces kadaifi pastry**
- 24 **large fresh basil leaves**

2 hours in advance

Combine the lemon juice, garlic, coriander and hot sauce in a bowl, add the shrimp and coat well, then cover and refrigerate for 2 hours.

To make the tarator

Soak the bread in a bowl of water, then squeeze out the excess. Place the bread in a food processor with the pine nuts, parsley, lemon juice and garlic. Process to a smooth puree, and slowly drizzle in the olive oil. Season, and refrigerate until needed.

To cook the shrimp

Pour enough oil into a large saucepan to come halfway up the sides and heat over high heat to 375°F. Cut the kadaifi into 12 strips, each about 4 inches wide. Lay out a pastry strip and arrange 2 basil leaves on top. Place a marinated shrimp on one end and roll the pastry around it. Repeat with the remaining ingredients. Deep-fry the shrimp for about 3 minutes, until golden brown. Using a slotted spoon, transfer to paper towels to drain for 1 minute. Serve with the tarator.

SERVES 4

Cumin and Sumac Crusted Sea Bass

Cumin and sumac are among the most popular spices in the Eastern Mediterranean, and when used together they complement each other beautifully. Cumin gives depth and warmth, sumac adds lemony notes.

sea salt and freshly ground pepper

8 skinless sea bass fillets (about 4 ounces each)

2 tablespoons grapeseed oil

3 tablespoons cumin seeds, toasted and crushed

1 teaspoon crushed sumac

2 shallots, chopped

½ cup dry white wine

2 tablespoons chopped fresh chives

2 tablespoons chopped fresh oregano

Season both sides of the sea bass fillets. Brush with a little of the grapeseed oil and sprinkle with the cumin and sumac.

Lightly oil a nonstick pan with the remaining grapeseed oil and cook the fish over high heat for 2 minutes on each side. Remove from the pan and set aside. Add the shallots to the pan, sauté for 2 minutes, then pour in the wine, and cook until the liquid has reduced to less than half. Stir in the fresh herbs, and season.

Serve 2 sea bass fillets per person, drizzled with the pan sauce, and accompany with Avocado and Sumac Whip (page 66).

SERVES 4

Monkfish Shawarma

You might not think you know what shawarma is, but you do! Shawarma, *or* chevirme, *comes from the Turkish meaning "turning," hence the shawarma is the revolving meat on a vertical spit cooker seen in just about every Turkish restaurant. Sliced and served with salad in a flat bread, shawarma is the best-loved fast food of the Eastern Mediterranean.*

This recipe is prepared with monkfish instead of the more traditional chicken or lamb. It was given to me by the head chef of Al Halabi, Four Seasons, in Damascus, for which I am most grateful. You can make this with any meaty white fish.

FOR THE MARINADE

¼ **cup orange juice**

2 **tablespoons lemon juice**

1 **tablespoon ground coriander**

1½ **teaspoons chili paste, such as Chinese chili-garlic sauce**

2 **garlic cloves, minced**

1 **teaspoon ground cumin**

½ **teaspoon ground cardamom**

¼ **teaspoon ground turmeric**

FOR THE MONKFISH

1¼ **pounds monkfish fillets, cut into 1½-inch chunks**

Baba Ganoush (page 53), for serving

1 day in advance

Combine the orange juice, lemon juice, coriander, chili paste, garlic, cumin, cardamom and turmeric in a large bowl. Add the monkfish and coat well. Cover the bowl and refrigerate overnight.

To serve

Build a hot fire in an outdoor grill. Grill the monkfish, turning occasionally, about 4 minutes, until barely opaque when pierced with the tip of a knife. (Or, broil the monkfish.)

Serve hot, with the baba ghanoush.

SERVES 4

Crispy-Coated Whitebait with Quince Aïoli

Crispy-coated whitebait is a favorite dish all over Istanbul. Aïoli is a Mediterranean type of sauce made with raw eggs, garlic and olive oil. Here I have added a fruity twist using cooked quince to create a tangy aïoli, which works really well with the fish. Make sure you use fresh, free-range eggs for the aïoli.

FOR THE AÏOLI

- 1 **large quince, peeled and grated**
- ½ **teaspoon sugar**
- 1 **garlic clove, minced**
- 2 **large egg yolks**
- 1 **tablespoon lemon juice**
- ½ **teaspoon Dijon mustard**
- ½ **cup olive oil**

FOR THE WHITEBAIT

- **vegetable oil, for deep-frying**
- ¼ **cup all-purpose flour**
- 1 **teaspoon crushed sumac**
- **sea salt and freshly ground pepper**
- 1¾ **pounds fresh whitebait**

To make the aïoli

Place the grated quince and sugar in a small saucepan and pour in just enough water to cover the quince. Bring to the boil, then reduce to a simmer for 3–4 minutes. Drain and cool the quince. Place the garlic, egg yolks, lemon juice and mustard in a food processor. Process and slowly drizzle in the oil. Transfer to a bowl. Fold in most of the quince, top with the remainder, cover and refrigerate.

To cook the whitebait

Pour enough oil to come halfway up the sides of a large saucepan and heat over high heat to 375°F. Place the flour and sumac in a bowl, season, and stir to combine. Coat the whitebait with the flour mixture, shake off the excess and deep-fry for 2–3 minutes, until golden brown. Using a slotted spoon, transfer the whitebait to paper towels to drain. Serve hot, with the aïoli.

SERVES 4

Grilled Baby Red Mullet Wrapped in Fresh Vine Leaves with Toasted Citrus and Nasturtium Flower Aïoli

This particular aïoli is flavored with fragrant toasted citrus peel and nasturtium flowers. It is the perfect accompaniment to simple grilled fish. Having spotted some baby red mullet at the fish market, I couldn't resist trying this combination.

FOR THE AÏOLI

- 2 **oranges**
- 1 **lemon**
- 1 **lime**
- 2 **large egg yolks**
- ½ **cup olive oil**
- ¼ **cup sunflower oil**
- **sea salt and freshly ground pepper**
- 1 **teaspoon Dijon mustard**
- 1 **shallot, finely grated**
- 1 **garlic clove, minced**
- 1 **tablespoon lemon juice**
- 5–7 **orange or yellow nasturtium flowers**

FOR THE MULLET

- 40 **vine leaves, fresh or preserved**
- 1¾ **pounds baby red mullet, cleaned heads left on**
- 3 **tablespoons olive oil**

- **crusty bread, for serving**

To make the aïoli

Preheat the oven to 225°F.

Using a vegetable peeler, remove the zest from the oranges, lemon, and lime and mince the zests. Spread the zests on a baking sheet lined with parchment paper. Bake for 15 minutes, until lightly toasted. Let cool.

Place the egg yolks in a food processor. With the machine running, slowly drizzle in the olive and sunflower oils until thick and creamy. Season, and combine with the mustard, shallot, garlic, lemon juice and toasted citrus zest. Serve topped with the nasturtium flowers.

To cook the mullet

Bring a saucepan of water to a boil. Add the leaves and cook 30 seconds for preserved leaves and 5 minutes for fresh. Drain and pat dry with paper towels. Preheat the broiler. Take one of the fish and wrap it with 2 or 3 vine leaves, then brush the parcel with some olive oil. It's a bit fiddly but ideally you need to completely enclose the fish by rolling the leaves around it and tucking the edges in. Repeat with the remaining leaves and fish. Grill for 3–4 minutes on each side, until the leaves are lightly charred.

Serve with the aïoli and bread.

SERVES 4

VEGETABLES

The shops abounded with fruit and vegetables. The peaches, nectarines and apricots were excellent; a species of the latter, which they call lousi, possessed the most exquisite and delicious flavour. What we found most agreeable of all was the great abundance of iced water that was exposed for sale in every quarter of the town. It is generally mixed with the fruit of figs or currants, and forms an agreeable and refreshing beverage, in which the Damascenes indulge to profusion.

Of the shopkeepers, I would say in general, that I never saw a more comfortable class of people in their station in life. They are clean, well dressed, of an excellent habit of body, and so extremely civil to strangers, that if they do not have the article which you wish to purchase, they will, unsolicited, walk with you to the place where you can be suited, and not leave until you say, "This will do: this is good."

Travels Along the Mediterranean, Robert Richardson, M.D. (1822)

Father's Eggplant Börek

*"Why," my editor asked, "is this recipe not in the section with the other böreks?"
The reason is simple: It is not really a börek at all, as it has no pastry, but it
was a dish my father loved making more than any other; it was his börek and
I cannot find it in my heart to change the name. I suppose he called it that
because when the eggplant is cooked with the eggs and flour it makes a kind
of fluffy batter, not so unlike a very light dough. Crispy on the outside and
meltingly mellow on the inside, this dish is a little tricky, but the final result is
very special.*

2 **large eggplants**

**sea salt and freshly ground
pepper**

11 **ounces feta**

5 **eggs, 2 beaten**

¼ **cup finely chopped fresh
mint**

⅓ **cup all-purpose flour**

2 **cups fresh bread crumbs**

1 **cup skinned and finely
chopped hazelnuts**

2 **tablespoons olive oil, as
needed**

**Tahini, Lemon and Sumac
Sauce (page 25)**

lemon wedges, for serving

Cut each eggplant into 12 rounds. Place in a colander and sprinkle
liberally with salt. Let stand for 20 minutes. Rinse under cold
water and dry with paper towels.

Meanwhile, make the filling: Mash the feta in a large bowl with a
fork. Mix in the 2 beaten eggs and the mint, and season with salt
and pepper.

Lay an eggplant round on your work surface and spoon on some of
the feta mixture, pressing down gently. Top with another eggplant
round to make a sandwich. Repeat with the remaining eggplant
and feta mixture until you have 12 "börek" sandwiches.

Using three dishes, put the flour in one, beat the remaining 3
eggs in the second and combine the bread crumbs and chopped
hazelnuts in the third. Coat each sandwich in the flour, then
coat in egg, and finally give them a good coat of the bread crumb
mixture.

Heat the olive oil in a large nonstick skillet over medium heat. Fry
the sandwiches on both sides for 3–4 minutes, until they're golden
brown and crisp, adding more oil as needed. Using a slotted spoon,
transfer them to paper towels.

Serve with the tahini, lemon and sumac sauce and the lemon
wedges.

SERVES 4

Mung Beans with Caramelized Onions and Nigella Seeds

The preparation of this dish could hardly be easier. It is one of the most loved salads on the menu of the Ciragan Palace in Istanbul. If you have never tried mung beans, this is a perfect introduction to these wonderful emerald-green pulses.

9 ounces dried mung beans, soaked in cold water overnight

½ cup olive oil

3 large onions, finely sliced

4 shallots, finely chopped

3 tablespoons red wine vinegar

2 tablespoons finely chopped fresh parsley

½ teaspoon Dijon mustard

sea salt and freshly ground pepper

8 sun-dried tomatoes, finely chopped

1 tablespoon nigella seeds, toasted

Drain the mung beans. Place in a saucepan and cover with cold water. Bring to a boil. Reduce to a simmer and cook for 30 minutes, until tender. Drain in a wire sieve.

Meanwhile, heat ¼ cup of the oil in a large saucepan over low heat. Add the onions and sauté for 20–25 minutes, until they are soft and lightly golden.

Combine the remaining ¼ cup oil with the shallots, vinegar, parsley and mustard in a bowl, and season. Add the warm mung beans and toss in the sun-dried tomatoes. Top with the cooked onions. Sprinkle with the nigella seeds.

Serve hot or cooled to room temperature.

SERVES 6

Sweet Roasted Peppers on Smoked Eggplant Puree

A smoky, smooth and creamy eggplant puree is a perfect base for sweet roasted red peppers. You can, if you wish, add some grated feta to the eggplant for a richer taste.

8 **long red bell peppers**

3 **tablespoons olive oil**

sea salt and freshly ground pepper

2 **medium eggplants**

juice of 1 **lemon**

2 **tablespoons unsalted butter**

¾ **cup coarsely chopped walnuts**

2 **tablespoons thick yogurt**

6 **ounces arugula**

Preheat the oven to 425°F.

Clean the peppers, removing the stems and seeds, and slice open lengthwise. Arrange them on a baking sheet and drizzle with the olive oil. Season and roast for 20–25 minutes, until tender. Cut the peppers into ½-inch-wide strips.

Place the eggplants directly on an open gas burner (or on an electric burner) and, taking care, cook over medium heat for 10–12 minutes, turning occasionally so that the eggplants are charred evenly. The skin will blacken and start blistering and the eggplants will become soft, not to mention that your kitchen will be filled with a wonderful smell. Alternatively bake them in the oven for 10–12 minutes, but the flavor won't be quite the same. Once cooked, place the eggplants in a strong plastic bag and allow to sweat, which will make them easier to peel.

Prepare a bowl of water with the lemon juice and keep it nearby. Peel the eggplants and discard the skin. Slice the flesh into very thin strips. Any uncooked eggplant should be discarded. Place the eggplant in the lemony water and soak for around 30 minutes. This is what gives the cooked eggplant its characteristic creamy white color.

Drain the eggplant flesh, discarding the water. Squeeze dry, place in a bowl and mash with a fork. Set aside.

Melt the butter over medium heat in a nonstick skillet and toast the walnuts for 2 minutes. Add the mashed eggplant and cook 2–3 minutes more, stirring all the time. Remove from the heat and stir in the yogurt, and season. Serve the puree topped with the pepper strips and arugula.

SERVES 4

Sumac Roasted Tomatoes with Dried Currants

This is one of the most underrated dishes, but the sweet combination of tomatoes and currants is delicious. Serve with lots of crusty bread for dipping.

8 plum tomatoes, halved, or 11 ounces vine cherry tomatoes

½ cup packed fresh basil leaves

4 shallots, finely chopped

4 garlic cloves, thinly sliced

2 teaspoons light brown sugar

1 teaspoon crushed sumac

½ teaspoon ground cinnamon

sea salt and freshly ground pepper

3 tablespoons olive oil

⅓ cup dried currants

Preheat the oven to 300°F.

Place the tomatoes, cut sides up, in a shallow roasting pan. Combine the basil, shallots, garlic, brown sugar, sumac and cinnamon in a bowl, and season. Scatter this mixture over the tomatoes and drizzle the olive oil over the top. Place in the oven and immediately reduce the heat to 275°F. Bake for 50 minutes.

Remove the roasting pan from the oven and scatter the currants on top. Return to the oven and bake for 20 minutes more, until the tomatoes are soft and slightly caramelized.

Serve warm or at room temperature with crusty bread.

SERVES 4

Eggplant Stacks with Pomegranate, Mint and Yogurt Sauce

This is a stunning-looking dish. Cooking the eggplants so that they are light and crispy is a must, so once they have been fried, drain them on paper towels to remove the excess oil. You can substitute pumpkin for the sweet potato if you prefer.

FOR THE SAUCE

- ¾ cup Suzme (page 22)
- 2 tablespoons finely chopped fresh mint
- 1 garlic clove, minced

seeds from
- 1 pomegranate
- 1 tablespoon Pomegranate Molasses (page 249)

FOR THE STACKS

- 1¾ pounds sweet potatoes, peeled and coarsely chopped
- sea salt
- 2 small eggplants
- freshly ground black pepper
- all-purpose flour, for dusting
- 2 tablespoons olive oil, as needed
- 1 tablespoon butter
- 5 ounces feta, coarsely chopped
- 2 tablespoons finely chopped fresh mint

seeds from
- 1 pomegranate, for garnish

To make the sauce

Combine all the ingredients together and refrigerate until needed.

To make the stacks

Place the sweet potato chunks in a saucepan, cover with water and bring to a boil. Add ½ teaspoon of salt and simmer gently for 15 minutes, until the potatoes are tender. Drain and set aside.

Cut the eggplants into sixteen ¼-inch-thick rounds. Season lightly with salt and pepper, and dust with flour. Heat the oil in a nonstick skillet and fry the eggplant for 3–4 minutes over medium heat, until golden on both sides, adding more oil as needed. Place on paper towels to drain.

Melt the butter in a saucepan and add the cooked sweet potato, feta and mint. Cook for 1–2 minutes to combine, then remove from the heat.

Preheat the oven to 425°F.

Line a baking sheet with parchment paper. Alternately layer the eggplant slices and potato mixture in 4 neat piles, starting with the largest slices at the bottom and finishing with the smallest slices on top. Bake for about 5 minutes, until heated through.

Serve hot, with the cold pomegranate sauce and garnished with pomegranate seeds.

SERVES 4

Go back as far as you will into the vague past, there was always a Damascus. To Damascus years are only moments, decades are only flitting trifles of time. She measures time not by days, months and years, but by the empires she has seen rise and prosper and crumble to ruin. She is a type of immortality. She saw Greece rise, and flourish two thousand years, and die. In her old age she saw Rome built, she saw it overshadow the world with its power; she saw it perish . . . She has looked upon the dry bones of a thousand empires and will see the tombs of a thousand more before she dies.

The Innocents Abroad, Mark Twain (1869)

Cumin-Scented Broth of Celeriac, Zucchini and Orange

A light and fragrant summery dish, this could be served as either a healthy starter or a main course – a feast for the eyes and the tastebuds! Eastern Mediterranean cuisine boasts a number of similar dishes, all of which burst with the flavor of seasonal produce.

1¾ **pounds celeriac (celery root), peeled and cubed**

1 **medium zucchini, peeled and cubed**

1 **Granny Smith apple, cored, peeled and quartered**

3 **celery ribs, chopped, leaves reserved**

juice of 1 **lemon**

1 **orange, halved**

3½ **cups vegetable stock**

4 **garlic cloves, peeled**

1 **tablespoon honey**

1½ **teaspoons cumin seeds, toasted and crushed**

3 **tablespoons olive oil**

sea salt and freshly ground pepper

Place the celeriac, zucchini, apple, celery, lemon juice and orange halves in a saucepan with the stock. Bring to a boil, then reduce to a simmer. Now add the peeled whole garlic, honey and cumin. Cook for 30–35 minutes over low heat, until the celeriac and zucchini are tender. Finally, add the olive oil, and season to taste. Remove the orange halves and discard.

Serve the broth hot in deep serving bowls, topped with a few celery leaves.

SERVES 4

Mahluba Rice with Eggplant, Topped with Feta and Pomegranate Seeds

Mahluba, a preparation of rice baked in the oven, is prepared for the kitchen staff at the Al Halabi, Four Seasons, in Damascus. I think that the guests should feel cheated, for this is not on the restaurant menu.

1 **medium eggplant**

1 **tablespoon vegetable oil**

1 **tablespoon clarified butter or ghee**

1 **large onion, finely chopped**

1 **garlic clove, minced**

¼ **cup olive oil**

1 **cup Arborio rice**

½ **teaspoon sweet paprika**

    sea salt and freshly ground pepper

2 **cups chicken stock**

7 **ounces feta, cubed**

seeds from 1 **large pomegranate**

Preheat the oven to 350°F.

Peel the eggplant and slice into ¼-inch-thick rounds, then halve each slice to make a half-moon shape. Heat the vegetable oil and butter over medium heat in a flameproof casserole. Fry the eggplant for 3–4 minutes, until golden brown. Transfer to paper towels to drain. Sauté the onion and garlic in the olive oil in the same casserole for 1–2 minutes. Add the rice and paprika and stir to coat well, then season. Add the eggplant and pour in the stock. Cover and bake for 15–18 minutes, until the rice is tender.

Serve hot, topped with chunks of feta and scattered with pomegranate seeds.

SERVES 8

Poached Asparagus with Nasturtium Sauce

*Eastern Mediterranean cuisines often make use of flowers and blossoms –
they add not only flavor but perfume and color too. Nasturtiums, the most
common of the edible flowers, can be grown in the garden during the summer
or ordered from a specialty grocer. They look stunning and have a slightly
peppery flavor, not dissimilar to watercress. They are delicious in salads and
pasta dishes, and also work very well when added to butter, as in this recipe.*

4 ounces fresh nasturtium flowers, plus 6 flowers left whole, for garnish

¾ cup vegetable stock

8 tablespoons unsalted butter, melted

1 pound fresh asparagus, trimmed and peeled

sea salt and freshly ground pepper

Remove the stems from the nasturtiums, then place the flowers in a bowl and pour boiling water over them. Let stand for 30 seconds, drain and place in a food processor. Add 3 tablespoons of the vegetable stock and pulse until pureed. Sit a small bowl over the top of a larger bowl that has been filled with ice cubes. Pour the puree into the smaller bowl. This will preserve the fresh and bright color of the flowers in the puree. Cool the puree completely, then return it to the food processor. Add the butter and process to combine.

Bring the remaining vegetable stock to the boil, then reduce to a simmer. Add the asparagus and cook for 3–4 minutes, until barely tender. Using a slotted spoon, divide the cooked asparagus among 6 dinner plates. Season the asparagus and top each with equal amounts of the nasturtium butter. Garnish with the nasturtium flowers and serve.

SERVES 6

SWEETS

My very own queen, my everything, my beloved, my bright moon;
My intimate companion, my one and all, sovereign of all beauties, my sultan.
My life, the gift I own, my be-all, my elixir of Paradise, my Eden,
My spring, my joy, my glittering day, my exquisite one who smiles on and on.
My sheer delight, my revelry, my feast, my torch, my sunshine, my sun in heaven;
My orange, my pomegranate, the flaming candle that lights up my pavilion.
My plant, my candy, my treasure who gives no sorrow but the world's purest pleasure;
Dearest, my turtledove, my all, the ruler of my heart's Egyptian dominion.
My Istanbul, my Karaman, and all the Anatolian lands that are mine;
My Bedakhshan and my Kipchak territories, my Baghdad and my Khorasan.
My darling with that lovely hair, brows curved like a bow, eyes that ravish:
I am ill. If I die, yours is the guilt. Help, I beg you, my love from a different religion.
I am at your door to glorify you. Singing your praises, I go on and on:
My heart is filled with sorrow, my eyes with tears.
I am the Lover – this joy is mine.

Suleiman the Magnificent (1494–1566),
written in honor of his favorite concubine, Roxelana

Rose and Champagne Jelly with Crystallized Rose Petals

Make sure you make this at least a day in advance so the jelly and rose petals have time to set.

petals of 1 **large unsprayed pink or red rose**

1 **egg white**

⅓ **cup superfine sugar**

FOR THE ROSE PETAL MASH

petals of 6 **unsprayed pink or red roses**

½ **cup superfine sugar**

grated zest
of 1 **small lemon**

FOR THE JELLY

3 **sheets gelatin (see note)**

6 **tablespoons superfine sugar**

1 **cup rosé champagne (or any sparkling rosé)**

6 **tall glasses, at least ½-cup capacity each**

To make the crystallized rose petals

Line a baking sheet with parchment paper. Wash the petals thoroughly. Brush each petal on both sides with egg white. Now carefully coat each petal with superfine sugar. Place on the baking sheet. Let stand overnight, until the petals are firm enough to pick up.

To make the rose petal mash

The rose petal mash will need to infuse for 2 hours before you add it to the jelly. Wash the petals, then place them in a bowl and sprinkle with the sugar and lemon zest. Using your fingers, rub the petals with the sugar until it all combines into a soft mass. Let stand for 2 hours.

To make the jelly

Soak the gelatin sheets in a little water to soften. Meanwhile, dissolve the sugar in 2¼ cups water in a medium saucepan over medium heat. Simmer for 5 minutes, then remove from the heat. Squeeze any excess water from the softened gelatin sheets and drop them into the hot sugar and water mixture. Stir until the gelatin dissolves. Mix in the champagne and the rose petal mash. Pour into the 6 tall glasses. Refrigerate overnight, until set.

Finish with a few crystallized rose petals.

SERVES 6

Note: Sheet gelatin makes the clearest jelly. It is available online at www.kingarthurflour.com and www.amazon.com and at well-stocked kitchenware stores.

Saffron and Pistachio Helva

In the fifteenth century, the palatial Ottoman kitchens were rebuilt to include a structure with six domes called the Helvahane, the House of Helva, where numerous varieties of helva, as well as jams, sherbets and herbal remedies, were made. By the mid-eighteenth century, the six different kinds of helva prepared in the Helvahane were assigned to different chefs, with a hundred apprentices working under each of them. Today, the preparation of helva still marks religious days and occasions such as births and deaths.

Helva is a dessert, a sweet made of semolina, flour, tahini or even vegetables, often enriched with dry fruits and nuts. Helva translates as "sweetmeat." My favorite is semolina helva and this recipe here was my father's; you can replace the saffron with vanilla pods as an alternative.

2 **cups milk**

½ **teaspoon saffron threads, plus more for garnish**

1 **cup granulated sugar**

6 **tablespoons unsalted butter**

1 **scant cup semolina**

¾ **cup pistachios, lightly toasted**

Heat 2 tablespoons of the milk. Add ½ teaspoon of the saffron and let stand for 30 minutes.

Stir the remaining milk with the sugar in a saucepan over medium heat until the sugar dissolves. Keep warm. In a separate heavy saucepan, melt the butter. Add the semolina and stir constantly over low heat for 20–25 minutes, watching carefully, until the semolina turns golden brown.

Stir the saffron-infused milk into the warm milk and sugar mixture, and add to the semolina, stirring vigorously until combined. Turn off the heat, cover and let the helva rest in a warm spot for at least 15 minutes.

Rub off as much skin as you can from the toasted pistachios. Grind in a food processor. Serve the helva at room temperature, sprinkled with the ground pistachios and garnished with a few saffron threads.

SERVES 6

Orange and Hazelnut Cake with Orange Flower Syrup

This is a wheat-free cake, very light and fluffy, soaked in a zesty syrup. Cakes are not as popular as filo pastries in the Eastern Mediterranean, but this is a specialty of the Jewish quarter on the Asian side of Istanbul.

FOR THE SYRUP

- 1¼ **cups superfine sugar**
- 2½ **tablespoons orange juice**
- 2½ **tablespoons orange flower water**
- grated zest of 1 **orange**

FOR THE CAKE

- 5 **large eggs, separated**
- 1 **cup superfine sugar**
- 2¼ **cups hazelnut flour or meal**

TO SERVE

- 1⅓ **cups Greek-style yogurt**
- 2 **tablespoons confectioners' sugar**
- pulp of 4 **passion fruits**

  8 x 4-inch loaf pan

Preheat the oven to 350°F.

To make the syrup

In a saucepan, bring ⅔ cup water to a boil. Add the sugar and orange juice and simmer for 10–12 minutes, until the sugar has dissolved and the mixture is thick and syrupy. Remove from the heat and let cool. Stir in the orange flower water and orange zest.

To make the cake

In a bowl, with an electric mixer on high speed, beat the egg yolks with the sugar until thick and pale. Fold the hazelnut flour into the yolk mixture. In a separate bowl, whisk the egg whites until stiff and glossy, then gently fold them into the hazelnut mixture.

Grease the loaf pan and line with parchment paper. Pour in the batter. Bake for about 30 minutes, until lightly golden. Remove the cake from the oven and evenly pour the cooled orange syrup over the top.

To serve

Combine the yogurt, confectioners' sugar and passion fruit pulp in a bowl. Serve generously with the warm cake.

SERVES 8–10

Pistachio Revani with Passion Fruit Syrup

This is another recipe that brings back fond memories of my childhood. Revani, a soft semolina cake, is sticky and delicious. This is a modernized version.

FOR THE SYRUP

1¾ cups **superfine sugar**

pulp of 10 **passion fruits**

FOR THE REVANI

6 **tablespoons unsalted butter, softened**

⅓ cup **superfine sugar**

2 **large eggs, separated**

½ cup **finely chopped pistachios**

¼ cup **all-purpose flour**

½ teaspoon **baking powder**

½ cup **semolina**

TO SERVE

pulp of 4 **passion fruits**

⅔ cup **mascarpone**

¾ cup **chopped pistachios**

8-inch round cake pan

Preheat the oven to 375°F.

To make the syrup

Combine the sugar, passion fruit pulp and 1⅔ cups water in a saucepan and bring to a boil over medium-high heat. Reduce the heat and simmer for 15 minutes, until syrupy and reduced by almost half. Let cool.

To make the revani

Lightly grease the cake pan.

Beat the butter and sugar in a bowl until light and creamy. Add the egg yolks and fold in the pistachios, flour and baking powder. Gradually add the semolina and mix for 1–2 minutes to combine well. Whisk the egg whites until stiff and glossy, and gently fold them into the cake batter. Spread the batter in the pan. Bake for about 25 minutes, until just lightly golden on top. Remove from the oven, pour the cooled passion fruit syrup evenly over the top and allow to soak well.

To serve

Combine the passion fruit pulp and mascarpone in a bowl. Cut the cake and serve warm, with a spoonful of passion fruit mascarpone and with chopped pistachios scattered on top.

SERVES 6–8

Maple Glazed Roasted Figs with Pistachio Praline

FOR THE PRALINE

²/₃	cup toasted and coarsely chopped pistachios
4	teaspoons superfine sugar
2	teaspoons unsalted butter, softened

FOR THE FIGS

12	large figs
4	tablespoons unsalted butter, melted
juice of 2	pomegranates
¼	cup maple syrup
1½	tablespoons Pomegranate Molasses (page 249)
seeds from 10	cardamom pods, ground

Preheat the oven to 375°F.

To make the praline

Mix the pistachios, sugar and butter in a small bowl. Line a baking sheet with parchment paper. Spread the pistachio mixture evenly on the baking sheet. Bake for about 8 minutes. Turn off the heat and let stand in the oven while the praline cools. Remove the cooled praline from the oven and break into small pieces with a rolling pin.

To cook the figs

Reheat the oven to 350°F.

Trim the figs and cut a cross into the top of each, cutting halfway down into the flesh. Arrange them on a baking sheet and brush with the melted butter.

In a bowl, combine the pomegranate juice, maple syrup, pomegranate molasses and cardamom. Drizzle over the figs and bake for about 15 minutes, until tender and lightly caramelized.

Serve the figs straight from the oven, topped with the pistachio praline.

SERVES 4

Fig and Cardamom Ice Cream

*I just adore figs! Gooey and toffeelike, they make this ice cream a very beautiful
dessert indeed, particularly with the added hint of cardamom. Sometimes
I sprinkle on some caramelized pistachios before serving too. This can be served
on its own or to accompany a simple sponge cake.*

20 **fresh figs**

¾ **cup superfine sugar**

½ **cup heavy cream**

½ **cup half-and-half**

¼ **cup blood orange juice**

¼ **teaspoon cardamom seeds,
   ground**

Trim the figs, then, using a fork, roughly mash them, including
the skins if they're really fresh. Place the mashed figs in a
saucepan and add the sugar and 6 tablespoons water. Cook
over medium heat for 20–30 minutes, stirring from time to
time, until thick and jamlike. Add the heavy cream, half-and-
half, blood orange juice and cardamom.

Using an ice cream machine, churn the ice cream as per your
machine's instructions. Transfer the ice cream to a covered
container and freeze until firm enough to scoop, at least 2 hours.
(If you haven't got an ice cream machine, then place the mixture
in a plastic container, cover and freeze. You'll need to stir the ice
cream every half an hour for at least 4 hours.) Scoop into bowls
and serve.

SERVES 6

Pink Peppercorn and Cardamom Meringues with Mulberries and White Chocolate

This is one of my all-time favorite recipes. The delicate pink peppercorn meringues are delightfully crisp and spicy, perfect with the tangy berries. Pink peppercorns are very much loved in Turkish cuisine, being both light and fragrant. Mulberries were what I found in season when I was working on this recipe, but you can use whatever fresh berries you have available.

FOR THE MERINGUES

- 4 large egg whites
- 1 cup superfine sugar
- 1 teaspoon cornstarch
- ½ teaspoon white wine vinegar
- 1½ tablespoons pink peppercorns

TO SERVE

- 4 ounces white chocolate, finely chopped
- 4 ounces fresh mulberries, black or red raspberries, or blueberries
- ¼ teaspoon ground cardamom

To make the meringues

Preheat the oven to 275°F. Line a baking sheet with parchment paper.

Whisk the egg whites until they form stiff, glossy peaks. Whisk in the sugar, a little at a time, then fold in the cornstarch and vinegar. Make 6 large meringues by dropping large dollops of the egg white mixture onto the baking sheet. Grind the pink peppercorns with a mortar and pestle. Rub three-quarters of the ground peppercorns through a sieve over the top of the individual meringues. Cook for 1 hour without opening the door. When cooked, the meringues should be a firm and pale honey color. Turn off the oven and let the meringues cool completely in the oven.

To serve

Warm the chopped chocolate in a bowl over a pan of gently simmering water. Stir until all the chocolate has melted, and set aside. Place a meringue on a dessert plate and drizzle with some melted chocolate. Rub the remaining ground pink peppercorns through a sieve on top of the white chocolate, scatter on some berries, and sprinkle on a little cardamom. Serve immediately.

SERVES 4

Orange and Vanilla Crème Caramels

These need to be made 1 day in advance so that there's time to chill and set them in the fridge.

FOR THE CARAMEL

- ⅔ **cup superfine sugar**
- 2 **tablespoons orange flower water**

FOR THE CRÈME

- 1 **vanilla bean**
- 2⅓ **cups heavy cream**
- grated zest of 2 **oranges**
- ½ **cup superfine sugar**
- 2 **large eggs, plus 2 large egg yolks**
- 6 **(6-ounce) ramekins**

To make the caramel

Combine the sugar, ⅓ cup water and the orange flower water in a small saucepan. Cook over medium-low heat, stirring well until the sugar has dissolved. Increase the heat and cook until the sugar turns darker and caramelizes. Pour the caramel into the ramekins and let cool.

To make the crème

Scrape the seeds from the vanilla bean into a saucepan. Add the bean, cream and orange zest. Heat over low heat until steaming. Remove from the heat and let infuse for 30 minutes. Remove the vanilla bean.

Preheat the oven to 300°F.

In a large bowl, whisk the sugar, eggs and yolks together until thick and creamy. Slowly whisk in the cooled cream mixture. Pour into the ramekins and place them in a baking dish. Fill the dish with enough boiling water to come two-thirds of the way up the sides of the ramekins. Bake for 1 hour, until almost set. Remove from the oven and let the crème caramels cool in the water. Chill overnight to set.

SERVES 6

Künefe with Passion Fruit and Vanilla Syrup

A deliciously crunchy, creamy and sweet confection, made with finely shredded filo pastry baked until crisp and golden, then soaked in syrup. This is a very common sweet throughout the Eastern Mediterranean and the Middle East.

This particular recipe was given to me by the head chef of Al Halabi, Four Seasons, in Damascus, but instead of the local cheese, I've used a combination of mozzarella and mascarpone, which works just as well. Traditionally the syrup is simply made with sugar and water, sometimes flavored with rose water. This passion fruit syrup is a divine alternative!

FOR THE SYRUP

pulp of 6 **passion fruit**

1½ **cups superfine sugar**

grated zest
of 1 **orange**

seeds of 1 **vanilla bean**

FOR THE KÜNEFE

11 **ounces thawed kadaifi pastry**

10 **tablespoons clarified butter or ghee, melted**

11 **ounces mozzarella, cut into small cubes**

⅔ **cup mascarpone**

¾ **cup coarsely chopped pistachios**

2 **8-inch square pans**

To make the syrup

Pass the passion fruit pulp through a fine sieve. Discard the seeds but keep the juice. In a saucepan, bring the sugar and 3 cups water to the boil. Simmer over medium heat until the sugar is dissolved. Cook until the liquid has reduced by about half, about 20 minutes. Remove from the heat and add the orange zest, passion fruit juice and vanilla seeds, stirring well to combine. Let cool.

To make the künefe

Preheat the oven to 350°F.

Using a sharp knife, cut the kadaifi pastry into ½-inch squares. Place the pieces in a bowl and add about two-thirds of the melted butter. Mix well to combine. Take half the buttered pastry and press it down into the bottom of an 8-inch square baking pan to create a compact base. Set the second pan aside.

Combine the mozzarella and mascarpone in a bowl, and spread the mixture over the compressed kadaifi base. Top with the remaining kadaifi pastry, again pressing down onto the cheese. Drizzle with the remaining butter. Bake about 20 minutes, until golden brown.

Remove the künefe and carefully invert it into the second pan, so that the upper side is now on the bottom. Return to the oven and bake for 20 minutes more. Remove from the oven and evenly pour the cooled syrup all over the künefe.

Sprinkle with the pistachios, cut into 4 squares and serve.

SERVES 4

Rose Petal Ice Cream

1¼ cups superfine sugar

petals of 6 large unsprayed red roses, rinsed

1 cup heavy cream

1 cup milk

5 large egg yolks

Place the sugar and the petals of 5 roses in a food processor and pulse to make a puree. Pour the heavy cream and milk into a saucepan and add the rose petal mixture. Bring to a simmer over medium heat, stirring until the sugar is dissolved. Remove from the heat.

Whisk the egg yolks and slowly beat in the hot cream mixture. Return to the saucepan and stir constantly over medium heat until it is thick enough to coat the back of a wooden spoon. Strain through a fine wire sieve into a bowl and let cool. Finely chop the petals of the remaining rose and add to the custard.

Using an ice cream machine, churn the ice cream as per your machine's instructions. Transfer to a covered plastic container and freeze until firm enough to scoop, at least 2 hours. Scoop into bowls and serve.

SERVES 6

Istanbul Orange and Vanilla Baklava

This, in my opinion, is the undisputed queen of baklava. It is even rare in Istanbul, being prepared only in one or two of the finest eateries. I tasted it for the first time last year in a restaurant in Istanbul and I was just blown away – I'd never had anything like it! The lush creamy and zesty orange layer, sandwiched between the golden crispy filo sheets, veiled in voluptuous and rich sugar syrup, is too amazing to describe. The moment I tasted this stunning dessert, I knew that it would become part of my life and I wanted to be able to prepare it for all those I love, so I asked for the recipe . . . And I was refused! To refuse to share a recipe is something I have never come across – to me, cooking and eating is about sharing and generosity! Nevertheless, I kept on thinking about that baklava, and went back to try it again, so I could recall the flavors and textures and attempt to re-create it at home.

I failed to come across an "orange baklava" reference almost anywhere in my research, though I did find something very close. So armed with this and my memories, with some persistence and lots of testing, this recipe was the result. I hope you love it as much as I do!

FOR THE SYRUP

- 1¾ **cups superfine sugar**
- 1½ **tablespoons orange juice**
- 1½ **tablespoons orange flower water**

FOR THE BAKLAVA

- 2 **large oranges**
- 1 **tablespoon orange marmalade**
- seeds of 1 **vanilla bean**
- 16–20 **sheets of thawed filo**
- 10 **tablespoons unsalted butter, melted**
- ¾ **cup coarsely chopped pistachios**
- **mascarpone, for serving**

- **11½ × 8-inch baking pan**

To make the syrup

Combine the sugar, 1½ cups water and the orange juice in a saucepan and gently bring to the boil. Reduce the heat and simmer for 10–12 minutes, until the syrup becomes thick and glossy. Add the orange flower water and let cool.

To make the baklava

Bring a large saucepan of water to the boil and add the whole oranges. Simmer for 45–50 minutes, until the fruit is soft, making sure the oranges are covered by water at all times. Remove the oranges with a slotted spoon and let cool. Slice the oranges open and pick out the seeds, then transfer all of the cooked orange (including the skin) to a food processor and process to a smooth puree. Place the orange pulp in a muslin bag or cloth and squeeze out as much of the liquid as possible. Discard the liquid and put the orange pulp into a bowl. Add the orange marmalade and vanilla seeds and mix well.

Preheat the oven to 350°F.

Walnut and Rose Water Baklava

There are more baklava recipes than you can shake a stick at, and in the Eastern Mediterranean almost every family has its own version. Some are made with almonds, others with pistachios. This walnut recipe was my grandmother's and she prepared it every Christmas, made with the new nuts from the recent harvest.

Twelve days before the lavish dinner was served on the evening of the twenty-fourth, she would begin, for, so she said, this wonderful confection needed time to mature. The smell of it cooking drove me to distraction. Once cooled, the baklava was soaked in syrup, then covered with a cloth and placed in the larder (which was in fact bigger than the kitchen). No greater torture could have been devised; to know that the baklava was there but not to be allowed to have any was agony. Unable to resist any longer, one morning, before anyone else was out of bed, I sneaked to the larder, carefully opened the door, praying that it would not creak, uncovered the baklava and pulled a little piece from the middle (stupid girl!). Every morning until Christmas I did the same thing. At the end of the meal on Christmas Eve my grandmother brought in the baklava, whipped off the cloth with a flourish, et voilà . . . Gasps and horrified expressions – the baklava was filled with holes! All eyes turned to me.

FOR THE SYRUP

1¾ cups **superfine sugar**

1¼ cups **rose water**

grated zest and juice of 2 **lemons**

FOR THE BAKLAVA

14 **tablespoons clarified butter or ghee, melted**

16 **sheets of thawed filo**

1¼ cups **ground walnuts**

4 **cups coarsely chopped walnuts, as fresh as possible**

1 **cup superfine sugar**
unsprayed pink rose petals, rinsed, for garnish

13 × 9-inch baking pan

To make the syrup

In a saucepan bring 1½ cups water and the sugar to a boil. Reduce to a simmer and add the rose water. Simmer for 15 minutes, stirring often, so that the sugar dissolves and the syrup thickens. Add the lemon zest and juice, then let cool.

To make the baklava

Preheat the oven to 350°F.

Brush the baking pan with a little of the melted butter. Arrange a filo sheet in the bottom of the pan, then brush the top with butter and sprinkle with some of the ground walnuts. Cover with another filo sheet, brush with butter and again sprinkle with ground walnuts. Don't press the layers down, and repeat until you've used 8 sheets of filo. Filo pastry can dry out very quickly, so when you're not using it, cover with a damp towel.

Combine the chopped walnuts and sugar and sprinkle half of this on top of the eighth filo sheet. Cover with 8 more sheets of filo, buttering and sprinkling each layer with ground walnuts. The top layer should be buttered and sprinkled with the remaining walnut and sugar mixture. Using a sharp knife, cut the baklava into diamond shapes, the size of a generous mouthful. Spray with water to help crisp up the pastry when cooking. Bake about 40 minutes, until golden brown.

Remove from the oven and pour the cooled syrup over the pastry, making sure that it seeps into every little gap. Let rest for 48 hours in a cool, dry place.

Serve garnished with a few rose petals and accompanied by Turkish tea.

SERVES 12

Blood Orange and Vanilla Buttermilk Sherbet

Sherbet is a sweet icy drink from Turkey and Persia. To me it is synonymous with sweetness and purity – back home people often say that a child is "sweet as sherbet!"

1	**vanilla bean**
½	**cup sugar**
grated zest of 1	**blood orange**
1	**cup buttermilk**
⅓	**cup blood orange juice**

Remove the seeds from the vanilla bean, then place the bean and seeds in a saucepan with ⅓ cup water, the sugar and orange zest and bring to a boil. Let cool a little, then transfer to a bowl and refrigerate until thoroughly chilled.

Once the mixture is cold, remove the vanilla bean and add the buttermilk and orange juice. Churn in an ice cream machine until slushy.

SERVES 4

Yogurt Panna Cotta with Apricot Mousse

This will need to be prepared a day in advance to allow the panna cotta and mousse to set.

FOR THE PANNA COTTA

- 2 sheets gelatin (see page 215)
- 1 vanilla bean
- scant 1 cup heavy cream
- ¼ cup sugar
- 6 tablespoons Greek-style yogurt

FOR THE MOUSSE

- 3 very ripe apricots
- 1 tablespoon sugar
- 1¼ sheets gelatin (see page 215)
- 4 ramekins

To make the panna cotta

Soak the gelatin in a little water to soften. Remove the seeds from the vanilla bean, then place the bean and seeds in a saucepan with the heavy cream and sugar. Over low heat, gently heat until the cream comes to a boil. Squeeze any excess water from the softened gelatin. Remove the cream from the heat and whisk in the softened gelatin until it's dissolved. Pour into a clean bowl and let cool until warm. Whisk in the yogurt. Lightly oil the ramekins. Pour into the ramekins and refrigerate to set for at least 2 hours.

To make the mousse

Pit the apricots, then puree them in a food processor. Place half the apricot puree with the sugar in a saucepan over medium heat. Meanwhile, soak the gelatin in a little water. Squeeze out any excess water. Stir into the warm apricot puree until it dissolves, then add the rest of the puree. Transfer to a bowl and let cool, stirring from time to time so that it doesn't set.

Pour the mousse onto the chilled panna cotta, so that you have a thin layer on each portion. Cover and refrigerate to completely set overnight.

SERVES 4

Pistachio, Rose Water and Honey Ma'amoul Cookies

These filled ma'amoul cookies are really something else. Use the very best pistachios you can find.

2¾ cups all-purpose flour, plus more for dusting

11 tablespoons clarified butter or ghee, cooled

scant ⅓ cup warm (105°–115°F) water

⅓ cup superfine sugar

½ teaspoon dry active yeast

1⅓ cups coarsely chopped pistachios

2 tablespoons honey

1 tablespoon rose water

40–50 whole pistachios, for decoration

Preheat the oven to 425°F.

Place the flour and butter in a food processor and, using the plastic blade, pulse to combine. In a bowl, combine the warm water, sugar and yeast. Let stand 5 minutes, then stir to dissolve the yeast. Add the flour and butter mixture and use your hands to combine. It will feel rather wet and loose, but have faith – this is how it is supposed to be. Refrigerate the dough for 10 minutes.

Combine the chopped pistachios, honey and rose water in a bowl to produce a sticky mixture. Dust a little flour on the work surface. Divide the cookie dough into quarters. Using your hands, roll each piece into a sausage, roughly 1 inch in diameter. With a knife, cut the dough into 40–50 disks. Place a small dollop of the pistachio filling into the middle of each disk, pull up the sides of the dough and roll into a ball to enclose the filling. Slightly flatten the cookies back into disk shapes.

Arrange the cookies on a baking sheet and place a whole pistachio on top of each one. Bake for about 7 minutes. They're ready as soon as they turn golden brown in color. Keep an eye on them, as they burn easily.

Let cool completely. Store in an airtight container.

MAKES 40–50

Lemon Balm and Chamomile Crème Brûlée

If there is one smell that takes me back to my childhood years, it is the sweet smell of lemon balm. Almost once a week, without fail, our apartment was filled with its smell, as my mother either prepared an almond and lemon balm crème brûlée or made lemon balm cookies.

2 cups heavy cream

3 sprigs of fresh lemon balm

8–10 sprigs of fresh chamomile leaves

5 large egg yolks

½ cup superfine sugar

¼ cup demerara sugar

6 (6-ounce) ramekins

Preheat the oven to 300°F.

Put the cream into a small saucepan with the lemon balm and chamomile and bring to a boil. Remove from the heat and let the flavors develop for a few minutes. Discard the lemon balm and chamomile leaves.

In a separate bowl, whisk together the egg yolks and superfine sugar. Whisk in the warm cream mixture. Strain through a fine sieve into a pitcher.

Place 6 ramekins in a roasting pan. Pour the custard into the ramekins. Pour enough boiling water into the pan to come halfway up the sides of the ramekins. Bake for about 30 minutes. To be sure it's cooked, lightly shake a ramekin – the custard should be set and wobble a little but not appear liquid. Remove the ramekins from the pan and let cool.

Cover and refrigerate the custards for at least 4 hours before serving. Sprinkle some demerara sugar on top, and caramelize with a kitchen torch or broil until the sugar is melted and bubbling.

MAKES 6

Pistachio Frangipane Tart

This is something that I love making at home, having been inspired by the wonderful pistachios in Turkish cuisine. The pastry is light, flaky and crisp, and the pistachio frangipane is moist and almost creamy.

FOR THE PASTRY

- 9 tablespoons unsalted butter, softened
- ¼ cup superfine sugar
- 1 large egg, beaten
- 1½ cups all-purpose flour

FOR THE FILLING

- 1 cup unsalted butter, softened
- 1 cup plus 2 tablespoons superfine sugar
- 2 large eggs, beaten
- grated zest of 1 lemon
- 1¾ cups ground pistachios
- ⅓ cup all-purpose flour
- ¾ cup cherry jam
- ½ cup chopped pistachios

- 1 tablespoon confectioners' sugar, for dusting
- whipped cream, for serving

- 6 tartlet pans, 4 inches in diameter

At least 2 hours in advance

First, make the pastry: Beat the butter and sugar together until light and creamy. Beat in the egg, then fold in the flour. Combine well to make a dough. Wrap the dough in plastic wrap and refrigerate for 2 hours.

For the filling, beat the butter and sugar until light and creamy, then gradually add the eggs and lemon zest. Finally, stir in the ground pistachios and flour and mix well.

Preheat the oven to 350°F.

Roll the chilled pastry to a ⅛-inch thickness. Cut 6 rounds about 5 inches in diameter. Use these to line the tartlet pans, trimming off any excess pastry. Spread the cherry jam in the bottoms of the tarts and pour in the pistachio mixture. Scatter the chopped pistachios on top. Bake for about 35 minutes, until the surface is golden. Let cool on a rack. Remove the pans.

Dust with confectioners' sugar and serve with a dollop of cream.

SERVES 6

Rose Petal Jam

petals of
8–10 **young unsprayed roses**

2 **cups superfine sugar**

juice of 2 **lemons**

3 **tablespoons rose water**

6 **(8-ounce) sterilized glass jam jars with their lids**

2 hours in advance

Wash the petals, making sure that they are clean, de-stemmed and free of pollen. Place the petals in a bowl and sprinkle with the sugar. Using your fingers, rub the petals with the sugar until you have a soft mass. Let infuse for 2 hours.

Place the infused petals in a large saucepan and add 1 cup water. Stir and cook over low heat for 10–15 minutes, until the liquid becomes thick and syrupy. Remove from the heat and stir in the lemon juice and rose water.

Pour the jam into the hot jam jars. Seal, process in a boiling-water bath, remove and cool completely.

MAKES 6 (8-OUNCE) JARS

The Eastern Mediterranean Pantry

Aleppo pepper Mild, sweet, fruity and slightly smoky. You might have to look around for it, but it is available crushed in many Turkish and Middle Eastern food stores. If necessary substitute sweet Spanish pimentón de La Vera and a pinch of crushed hot chili flakes.

Baharat Also known as seven spice, this is a wonderfully warming and aromatic blend of spices that can be added to soups, tomato sauces, lentils and pilafs, and rubbed on fish, poultry and meat. Mix it with a little olive oil and it can be used as a marinade too. It can also be combined with sumac, saffron and turmeric. You can easily make this yourself or buy it ready-made in some supermarkets and Middle Eastern shops. Here's my version:

> 4 teaspoons sweet paprika
> 4 teaspoons ground cumin
> 4 teaspoons ground black pepper
> 1 teaspoon ground ginger
> 1 teaspoon ground cinnamon
> ½ teaspoon hot paprika
> ½ teaspoon ground coriander

Place the seven spices in a small jar, give it a good shake and there you have it.

Makes about ⅓ cup

Bulgur These cracked wheat grains come in four grinds, from fine to extra coarse; use fine for these recipes.

Cardamom, green "The queen of spices" is used in both savory and sweet cooking. The pods are discarded to reveal the flavorful tiny black seeds, which are then ground.

Feta I prefer Bulgarian (firm and not too salty) and then Greek feta.

Filo This paper-thin dough, essential to Greek cooking, is a fine substitute for Turkish yufka, which is thicker and not easy to find in the U.S. Use thin filo for börek and baklava, but thick filo (if you can find it) for larger pastries with heavy fillings. *Kadaifi* is shredded filo. Filo is usually sold frozen, although some Middle Eastern markets sell it already thawed. To thaw filo, refrigerate it in its box overnight. Do not thaw at room temperature, or the sheets will stick together. Once opened, leftover filo can be refrigerated for a week or so. When working with filo, cover the portion waiting to be used with a damp towel to discourage drying.

Hemp seeds I use a wide variety of seeds in my cooking. Hemp seeds have great health benefits, but if you can't find them, substitute sesame or another crunchy seed.

Nigella seeds These come from a flower that is a member of the buttercup family. They have a sharp, nutty, slightly peppery flavor. Make sure you toast them beforehand to release the flavors.

Olive oil Use good-quality extra virgin oil

Olive oil, extra virgin Use a good-quality extra virgin oil; there is no need to use estate-bottled oil for cooking, but you may want to use it for salads.

Orange flower water Also known as orange blossom water, distilled from orange peels. Use very little – too much and you will end up with a heavily perfumed dish.

Paprika The true aristocrat of spices, from the noble sweet varieties to the fiercely hot, a spice that I grew up with, that I understand and love. Hungarian and Spanish paprikas are excellent.

Peppercorns (black, white and pink) White and black peppercorns are both berries from the same *Piper nigrum* plant, but white are fully ripened, and black are picked green and then dried. Pink peppercorns are actually the dried fruit of the Brazilian rosebush, and not related at all to the others.

Pomegranate molasses A thick syrup, made from boiling down pomegranate juice and sugar. It is sweet and sour at the same time. Delicious as a dressing, for marinating meat, or added to slow-cooked stews. Pomegranate molasses is also great to make drinks with. Readily available at Mediterranean markets, but easy to make at home. Here is a homemade version:

> 1 quart bottled pomegranate juice
> ⅔ cup sugar
> ⅓ cup lemon juice

In a large, uncovered saucepan, over medium heat, stir all the ingredients until the sugar has completely dissolved. Reduce the heat to a simmer and cook for roughly 1 hour, or until the juice has a syrupy consistency and has reduced to roughly 1 cupful. Pour out into a jar. Allow to cool, then store in the refrigerator for up to 4 weeks.

Rose water Similar to orange water, this perfumed flavoring should be used in small quantities.

Saffron Can be bought as threads or powdered. Threads are the most expensive; a pinch of saffron is roughly 12 threads.

Sea salt Use the fine crystals.

Sesame seeds Very high in oil content, with a nutty aroma. They're used to make za'atar, tahini and helva.

Sumac You'll see this is a key ingredient for many of my recipes and fortunately it's more widely available now. Any good Middle Eastern food shop will sell it crushed. Sumac is the edible berry from a tree related to the mango. Sumac berries turn from dark pink to purple as they ripen. As they dry and harden, they become the size of peppercorns. Sumac has a fruity aroma and citrusy flavor. Great with fish, salads and in pilafs. Its beautiful purple color inspired the title of this book!

Tahini Sesame paste, used widely in Eastern Mediterranean and Middle Eastern cuisines. Stir well before using to incorporate the sesame oil layer that rises to the top. Refrigerate after opening, but bring to room temperature before using.

Za'atar Both a herb in its own right and a blend of dried herbs. Za'atar the herb has long green leaves and a thymelike flavor. It is sometimes called wild thyme in English, and it grows along the slopes of the Syrian-Lebanese mountains. The za'atar referred to in this book, however, is the dried herb blend and I've included a recipe below. It's also available ready-made in Middle Eastern shops and some supermarkets.

> 2 tablespoons dried oregano or thyme
> 2 tablespoons sesame seeds, lightly toasted
> 1 tablespoon crushed sumac
> 1 tablespoon dried marjoram
> ½ teaspoon salt

Mix together and store in a jar.
Try this: drizzle some bread with olive oil, sprinkle with za'atar and eat for breakfast.

In the Spice Cupboard

Here is a list of the essential dried herbs, spices and flowers used in Eastern Mediterranean cooking. Store them in airtight containers in a cool, dark place away from the kitchen stove. Rather than buying ground spices, which stale quickly, it is best to freshly grind whole spices in a mortar and pestle or a spice grinder just before use. Some spices are toasted in a skillet and cooled before grinding to bring out their essential oils and flavors. Be sure to buy culinary dried flower petals, and not those that have been preserved for potpourri and the like.

Allspice berries

Cardamom pods (see entry)

Cinnamon, ground

Coriander seeds

Cumin seeds

Fennel seeds

Ginger, ground (also fresh)

Hibiscus, dried

Lavender, dried

Marjoram, dried

Mustard, dry

Nigella seeds (see entry)

Oregano, dried

Paprika, sweet and hot (see entry)

Parsley, dried

Peppercorns, black, pink and white (see entry)

Rose petals, dried

Saffron (see entry)

Vanilla beans

Index

Acknowledgments

This work is the result of a long and pleasurable journey, and there are so many people that I would like to thank that it would be impossible to name them all, but in my heart I know them. Let me record my gratitude to the following: Martin Knaubert, at the Four Seasons in Damascus, and his team of chefs, especially head chef Mohamad Helal at the Al Halabi, Aleppo's best-kept secret; Mr. Ugur Alparslan, Tuğra restaurant chef, at Ciragan Palace in Istanbul; Musa Daðdeviren, owner of Çiya in Istanbul, and chef Kerem Delibalta; Richard Marston for the elegant book design; the classy and stylish Elif Gönensay in Istanbul, who welcomed us into her home and her heart, thanks for making it real; Felicity Blunt, for taking my hand and leading me to Random House, I am truly grateful; Caroline Gascoigne for making me feel like a real author.

My most special thanks go to Emma Rose for working above and beyond the call of duty, for loving and cherishing this work as much as I do, and to Jonathan (Jonny) Lovekin, without whom there would be no life on these pages . . .

and to my husband, Malcolm, without whom life wouldn't taste the same!